The
WEST HIGHLAND WHITE TERRIER

EDITED BY
GEOFF CORISH

BEST of
BREED

ACKNOWLEDGEMENTS

The publishers would like to acknowledge the following for help with photography: Hearing Dogs for Deaf People, Pets As Therapy, Gill Blower; Holly Barrington (McHolglyn); Tina Squires (Bellevue); Karen Kibble (Albacharm), Jane Kabel (Llovall Design), and with special thanks to Dawn Martin (Dawn's Highland Scots).

Cover photo: © Tracy Morgan Animal Photography (www.animalphotographer.co.uk)
page 2 © istockphoto.com/Steve Pepple; page 3 © istockphoto.com/Linda Mirro
page 37 © istockphoto.com/Waldemar Dabrowski; pages 56 and 88 © istockphoto.com/Richard Hobson
pages 72 and 120 © istockphoto.com/Sebastien Cote; page 130 © istockphoto.com/Todd McLean.

The British Breed Standard reproduced in Chapter 7 is the copyright of the Kennel Club and published with the club's kind permission. Extracts from the American Breed Standard are reproduced by kind permission of the American Kennel Club.

THE QUESTION OF GENDER
The 'he' pronoun is used throughout this book instead of the rather impersonal 'it', but no gender bias is intended.

First published in 2009 by The Pet Book Publishing Company Limited
Chepstow, NP16 7LG, UK.
Reprinted in 2011 and 2013 by The Pet Book Publishing Company Limited

ISBN
978-1-906305-15-4
1-906305-15-3

Printed and bound in China through Printworks Int. Ltd.

CONTENTS

GETTING TO KNOW THE WEST HIGHLAND WHITE TERRIER

Chapter 1

So, you are considering adding a West Highland White Terrier to your household and you need to know a bit more about the breed. Well, what can I say? I have owned Westies since 1969 and still share my life with them. I couldn't imagine ever being without one. For me, this is a very special breed – a big dog in a small frame. In other words, an ideal dog. Westies are so adaptable, seeming to take life as it comes, and they are so attractive, too. The Breed Standard, which is the written blueprint describing the 'ideal' specimen, states that the Westie should be: alert, gay, courageous, self reliant but friendly. Westies are happy dogs who take an interest in everything that is going on.

Westies are "naughty but nice." Their piercing dark eyes look at you, full of mischief, through the rough, white hair that covers their faces. A Westie will smile at you, but you can see that he is thinking of what to do next. His pricked, attentive ears and black nose are very expressive – he always looks ready for fun. The picture is completed with a compact body and a busy tail. I never get enough of looking at the way a Westie moves, with his erect tail above a rounded back end. The white coat and dark points also add to a very attractive picture.

WESTIE WAYS

The Westie's rough and ready constitution, plus plucky character, goes back to the origins of the breed. The West Highland White Terrier's forbearers were spirited workers who earned their keep by their abilities, fearlessness, strength and tenacity. The dogs hunted marauding animals that competed with the people for game, which was needed for food. Usually working in a craggy terrain, a Westie could take out badger, fox and otter, as well as smaller vermin.

Well regarded for their gameness, Westies are known for possessing "no small amount of self esteem". In everyday life this means a Westie thinks he is as big as the really big dog he comes across on his daily walk. He knows little fear, and that sometimes can be a disadvantage if a bigger breed of dog doesn't realise how tough a Westie can be. There is no doubt that a Westie can make friends with bigger breeds, but this depends on the nature and character of the breed in question. As a result of his working ancestry, a Westie is not likely to back down, as he would be in danger if he showed fear towards the animals he hunted. This is a dog with an

The Westie has total belief that he is a big dog, and is ready to take on all-comers.

inquisitive nature. A Westie likes to be in the front line, so he knows what is going on, and he will take on any trouble he meets.

I used to take my first two Westies for a walk in a local park and we would meet many types of dogs. The bigger the breed, the keener my dogs were to have a word and, often, take them on. They would approach a Great Dane from underneath so the poor dog wouldn't know which way to go.

Many years later, when I took four of my Westies for a visit to my parents' home, we went for a walk in a nearby wood. All of a sudden, the male, Mitch (a once-in-a-lifetime dog), went to the

right and the three girls went to the left. They circled around a big hunting type of dog, which, from a distance, almost looked like a deer. But my Westies had him cornered. Luckily, they obeyed my call and returned without doing him any harm – but it certainly showed how cleverly they had worked out a strategy.

Westies are amazingly agile, and I love to watch their antics – particularly when youngsters are playing. When I let our Westies run free on the grass area, they play lovely games of 'catch me if you can'. At times it looks like a big heap of Westies rolling about. But, equally, I love watching them asleep. Sometimes a Westie

sleeps in a little curl, with his nose buried in his coat, or with his head resting on his front paws; some will even sleep on their back with their feet in the air. Some of ours do this when we are at shows, while they are waiting for their turn in the ring. Young pups can be found in this position at a very early age; it is certainly a sign of a contented puppy or relaxed adult.

We allow dogs to get on the settee when we are relaxing in the evening, which they view as a special treat. But most go away after a while and all find a different place to sleep. Of course, if you do not want to share your sofa with a Westie, you can teach him

The active Westie is always ready for a game.

to go to his own bed. However, we like to have them with us and they say it is very therapeutic for human beings to stroke a dog.

West Highland White Terriers are great greeters and they make you feel as if you have been greatly missed – even if you have only been away for a couple of hours. Most Westies will jump up – but, clever dogs that they are, they usually know when someone needs to be treated with more care. Some give lots of big kisses, some just gentle little ones, and some don't kiss. But there is no doubt that a Westie loves to see his people

A Westie seems to have an instinct that tells him when you are sad and need his companionship. He seems to know that life is not always fun and that humans sometimes need to be comforted. A Westie

can do this just by being there – I do think they consider themselves as being human most of the time. When a Westie joins a new family, I always say it is like having a child. A Westie becomes so much a part of the family, he deserves – and even demands – the same attention as a child. A Westie is also very loyal and easily forgives our bad moods or bad days.

A Westie is very focused on his owner in an independent sort of way; he likes to be with you, but usually on his own terms.

Westies are not needy dogs, but they are dogs that won't be ignored. Alert and gay, they are always ready for a game. Happily, Westies will take whatever comes their way and will enjoy taking a short stroll with an older adult as much as

running around outdoors with children. The object of every Westie's game is companionship.

Westies don't like to be left on their own all day, but can be trained to be left for limited periods. It is important to start young with any training, including leaving a pup on his own. Couples who are out at work all day, do not, in my opinion, make suitable dog owners. Some boarding kennels now offer day care. As long as some days of the week are spent with the dog – and that time is quality time – I guess it would be all right. But a puppy needs training at first, so this arrangement would not be suitable for a young puppy. An older pup can be left on his own for a morning, as long as he has grasped the principles of house training. It is possible to own a

The Westie is very much a people dog and will not thrive if he is left for long periods on his own.

'terra', meaning earth – i.e., they go to ground. The Westie loves to dig; this is a deep-seated instinct that has been bred for over many generations and is still strongly in evidence today. You will need to abandon hopes of a beautifully manicured lawn if you own a Westie! He will also think nothing of digging out your precious plants or even tunnelling underneath the garden fence.

Some owners have found that a purpose-built sandpit is the best solution for a Westie that loves to dig. You could create a sand pit, but it should be covered when it is not in use, as sand attracts fleas brought in by stray cats and other animals. Another option is to fence off the flower borders from the grassy areas. Or, better still, fence off a patio with restricted access to the grass and the rest of the garden. It is possible to create a dog-friendly but pretty garden. Nowadays, there are even specialised designers just for that.

The hunting instinct is usually quite strong in a Westie. Generally speaking, the girls seem to be keener hunters than the boys. A Westie's natural response is to chase, as he sees any small, fast-moving animal as vermin. However, if a Westie is brought up with a cat, he will learn to respect it, and the two animals will live in harmony. However, rabbits and other small pets may be regarded as fair game. If you keep small animals as pets, they will need to be very safely confined if you have a Westie in the house.

Westie while working, but the dog's welfare should come first. A Westie depends on us – and this is a breed that loves human company.

WATCH DOG

Generally, Westies do not bark unless they have something to say. An attentive owner can distinguish what is intended by various barks. Most Westies are excellent watchdogs because their barks of alarm suggest a dog many times their compact size. Of course, if your watchdog is sitting in the window, the jig is up, so to speak! I have found some Westies are more alert than others, and some bark with a deeper voice when they hear something unusual.

INHERITED BEHAVIOUR

Westies are terriers, a word that derives from the Latin word

A compact, short-legged terrier, the Westie is a handy size for a pet dog.

PHYSICAL CHARACTERISTICS

Physically, the West Highland White Terrier is a short-legged, medium-sized terrier, similar to the Scottish and Cairn Terriers (with the Scottie being the heavier, and the Cairn being slightly lighter in weight). The story goes that a breeder selected the white-coated pups in his litters because he could see them better while hunting; the red-coated Cairn Terrier could be mistaken for a fox.

The Westie's medium size was required when he was going to earth in pursuit of badger or fox, but it also makes him an ideal pet, as he fits into any home and

is easy to take travelling. A Westie doesn't take up much room in the car, the train and the bus or at dog-friendly hotels – and you can always find a space for the dog to stretch his legs.

According to the Breed Standard, the height at the withers, which is the highest point of the shoulders, should be approximately 28 centimetres (11 inches). Weight is not mentioned in the Breed Standard, but it can vary from 7-12 kilos depending on the bone of the dog. Bitches usually weigh less than dogs.

The Westie has a compact body. It should be square, looking at it from the sides, with deep ribs, a level back, broad

loins, muscular hindquarters and strong legs. He has a broad skull, with a very powerful jaw, and teeth that are relatively large for the size of the dog, which were required for killing vermin.

Facial expression is very important to the breed. The dark eyes are widely set, almond-shaped, and medium in size. They have a piercing expression – a Westie doesn't miss a thing – which is of vital importance for a hunting dog. The small erect ears also contribute to the overall expression. When you look at a litter of Westie pups, you will find that not all pups have the erect ears that are so typical of the breed. This is nothing to

When you look at a litter of Westie pups, you may find that not all the puppies have the typical erect ear carriage – but this will change as the puppies grow.

long. This goes back to the breed's hunting days on rough terrain, where dogs needed the protection of their coat in all sorts of weather in the Scottish Highlands. Silky coats and curly coats are considered faults.

EXERCISING A WESTIE

With regard to exercise, Westies are ideal dogs. They love to go for walks but will also be content to race around the garden, playing ball; some even love playing fetch and never tire of the game. Of course, you can't expect a puppy to go for a long hike, but a fit adult Westie that is in good condition can walk long distances. It is great to have a big garden – but if you haven't, taking your Westie out for regular walks is just as good. Make sure you always clean up after your dog, as we don't want to give dogs a bad name.

As a student, I lived on the fourth floor in just one room with two Westies. I walked them a lot, taking them to the park, but they also loved it when I went to my parents' home. There we could go in the garden and we would take them to a big heath where they could run off the lead. When I travelled by train, they would sit in a wicker basket so they could travel for free.

In my experience, a Westie who gets plenty of exercise and fresh air will be fit and healthy, and will enjoy his life to the full. A Westie loves exercise, but he won't tear the house down or become difficult if, at times, he has to make do with less exercise.

LIFE EXPECTANCY

The average life expectancy of a Westie is said to be 11 years, but it isn't uncommon for them to live well into their late teens. Some stay very fit up until the end and don't really show their age. Of course, some dogs become frail, but they seem to stay tough for a long time. Being a white-coated breed, they don't show their age with greying hair, as some breeds do.

worry about – by 10 or 12 weeks the ears should be up, although occasionally the tips may come down when a pup is losing his baby teeth.

The Westie should have a short undocked tail that should be as straight as possible – but not carried gaily 'over the back'. Fortunately, Westies naturally have a short tail. In Europe, and now in the United Kingdom, the docking of tails is forbidden; in America, docking continues at the owner's discretion.

The Westie has a double white coat (a soft undercoat with a harsh outer coat) that should be pure white and straight. The coat should be approximately 5 cm (2 in)

This is a hardy dog that will enjoy exercise in all weathers.

A Westie can give a fair imitation of a couch potato on occasions.

THE WESTIE COAT

The Westie requires regular grooming; I advise new owners to get help with this from a professional groomer.

When a Westie is being exhibited in the show ring, he should be groomed every week, each time removing only a little bit of dead hair from the coat. Most show dog owners have learnt to do this themselves. Owners of pet Westies usually opt for having their dogs clipped; this should be done every six to eight weeks to keep the dog looking tidy. Please note that having the coat clipped will make it softer, thus ruining it for showing. A coat that is stripped (plucked) will be much harder and doesn't tend to get dirty as quickly as a clipped coat.

Sadly, many professional groomers do not have the time, inclination or knowledge to hand-strip, so the only option is to learn to do it yourself. As with all dogs, regular grooming and brushing is very important.

Now that we don't use our Westies for the job they were bred for, coats seem to have changed – and not for the better. A harsh double coat is what was needed; a soft coat that tangles easily was of no use to working dogs.

WESTIES AND CHILDREN

Westies can share a house with children, but I always maintain that it depends a lot on the parents and the kids. Westies, like all other dogs, are not toys for the children to do with whatever they wish. A child and a dog should never be left alone together. No matter how trustworthy a dog (of any breed) appears to be, you cannot predict what might happen – particularly if a dog feels cornered for some reason. All interactions should be supervised by a willing adult.

My Westies did not grow up with children, but my dear Coco just loved them. I always had to be watchful when I was showing her, to make sure no baby strollers were at the ringside. Her idea of fun was to go and greet the baby or toddler rather than strut her stuff in the show ring. She was one of my best West Highlands in terms of looks and temperament – and it is great when both qualities go hand in hand.

Don't expect a child to be able to train a Westie when he arrives in your home. A Westie is very much a pack animal and may see the children as members of his own pack. It is your job to be kind, but also firm and consistent, so that your Westie learns his place in the family group. It is very important for the new addition to know who is boss.

LIVING WITH OTHER DOGS

As Westies are inherently pack animals (there are exceptions), it is possible to have more than one dog in the same household. However, it is advisable to have a good difference in age between the dogs. Rearing and house training two pups from the same litter or age can be very difficult.

When you have two pups of the same age, a lot of training is required and the pups can get very confused. You will be telling one off because he is showing unwanted behaviour, and the other pup will get the same warning, which he won't understand. Pups of the same age also find mischief together, and they are good at teaching each other bad habits. Some people say that two pups grown up together are less human-orientated; maybe that is the case of other breeds, but I haven't found this to be true of Westies. We have had two pups that grew up together, and they loved us as much as any of the other dogs. But it was definitely more difficult

to house train them and teach them manners.

At the moment we have two bitch pups born on the same day from different litters. Interestingly, they are quite different in temperament and character. So far, Stitch and Chelsey are OK together, perhaps because they are different characters. However, there is always a chance that they will start to argue about dominancy. This may happen with two bitches, and if they take a dislike to each other, there is very little you can do, apart from rehoming one of them. But if there is a gap between the ages of the two dogs, a natural pecking order is established, and the two will live amicably together.

I am not sure if a Westie prefers to live with his own kind, or to share his life with a different breed. We had Samoyeds and Westies living together in our family home; they got on fine,

Westies enjoy each other's company, but you will make life easier for yourself if there is a reasonable age gap between the dogs.

but they seemed to stick with their own breed rather than mixing – I guess, size difference played a part. My first Westie disliked one Samoyed, as she was pulled about by a visiting Sammy puppy when young. The Sammy puppy was only playing, and Shinny was not hurt, but she never forgave him. Our own Westies seem colour-biased and can get worked up about different coloured breeds. However, Fling, who was brought up with Norfolk Terriers, was more than happy to greet any small brown-coloured dog.

Two Westies of the same sex will get on, but I find that a male and female together works best. Obviously, either one of the dogs (or preferably both) need to be neutered. Ask your vet to advise you on the best age for neutering. Westies can also share the house with a different and bigger breed of dog – but it is important that the bigger dog is of a kind and gentle breed. The Westie may be small, but he certainly doesn't think he is. Regardless of the size of his canine companion, a Westie will want to be the boss.

TRAINABILITY

The Westie has a very strong character and he needs an owner that does not indulge him too much! A Westie likes to do things in his own way and on his own terms. Given the chance, he will easily gain the upper hand and may show behavioural problems. Do not expect a Westie to "Heel" and "Sit" on command. A Westie will consider the request first, and then decide whether to obey or not… The Westie is a highly intelligent breed that is eager to learn, but he needs a patient and persistent trainer. A Westie has a great sense of humour and knows how to make the most of every situation; he is a natural crowd-pleaser.

If you are interested in taking on a challenge, a Westie can compete in a number of canine sports, such as obedience and agility, and in the USA the breed competes in earthdog trials and tracking events. See Chapter Six: Training and Socialisation.

SPECIAL SKILLS

Some Westies are more anxious to please than others – just as some breeds are more suitable for certain tasks than others – but Westies are very adaptable and have proved their worth in a number of roles.

SEARCH AND RESCUE

Search and rescue dogs are used where humans are lost or buried in the aftermath of an earthquake, an avalanche, or a collapsed building. They are also used to find mountain climbers

There is no doubt that the West Highland has a mind of his own.

Therapy dogs can brighten up the lives of the elderly or unwell.

who have lost their way. With a sense of smell far more powerful than a human's and an ability to probe nooks and crannies that people cannot penetrate, these dogs often save lives. The Westie can be trained to work in this sphere and has proved particularly useful working over rough terrain.

THERAPY DOGS
Adaptable and hardy, with a great love of people, the Westie makes an ideal therapy dog. Pets As Therapy (PAT) is a national charity that promotes the use of specially trained PAT dogs to visit hospitals and nursing and residential homes. The medical profession is increasingly aware of the therapeutic benefits of pets, particularly for children, people with mental illnesses and elderly people who may have been separated from their own pets. Stroking and playing with a pet is a calming and tactile experience and something to look forward to. One hospital reported that a man with a mental illness who hadn't spoken for years started talking to a visiting dog.

PAT dogs come in all shapes and sizes and range from mutts to Crufts Champions. Long-term patients and residents build up relationships with PAT dogs and, of course, PAT dog owners are willing listeners and enjoy hearing the residents talking about the memories of their own pets.

HEARING DOGS
Hearing dogs are trained to alert deaf or hearing-impaired people to the everyday sounds that hearing people take for granted, such as alarm clocks, doorbells, telephones, smoke alarms etc. The dogs are trained to communicate by touch, and then either lead to the sound source or lie down to indicate danger. Potential owners are carefully assessed as to the degree of their deafness and desire to look after a dog.

A hearing dog can transform the life of his deaf owner.

Benefits to those with hearing dogs include feelings of greater confidence, self-esteem and well-being; reduced stress; and encouragement to go out more often, to meet new people and take regular exercise.

Dogs can bring renewed interest in life and can result in a greater acceptance into the hearing community. Caring for dogs can increase the frequency of visitors and phone calls. Finally, the dogs provide constant and devoted companionship.

SUMMING UP

If you want a dog that doesn't need grooming, a Westie is not for you… If you are looking for a dog that will always be obedient, a Westie is not for you… But, if you are prepared to spend some time grooming your dog, taking him to a professional groomer, or learning to do the job yourself, a Westie is for you… If you are looking for a big dog in a small package – in other words, a small dog with a big heart – then a West Highland White Terrier is for you…

If you want a hardy dog that is lots of fun to have around and easy to live with when trained properly, a Westie is for you… If you can put up with a dog that likes to dig and doesn't mind getting dirty, and if you enjoy going for walks, the Westie is for you.

As we Westie lovers tend to say: if it is not a Westie, it is not a dog. Yes, I know I am biased, and other breed owners could be offended hearing me say this – but the Westie is something very special!

THE FIRST WEST HIGHLAND WHITE TERRIERS

Chapter 2

The islands that make up the British Isles are the natural home of the terrier. There are 23 different terrier varieties indigenous to these islands: 12 have very firm roots in England; two are from Wales; and four come originally from Ireland. However, our interest is in the five breeds of Scottish heritage. Four of these five breeds – the Cairn Terrier, the Skye Terrier, the Scottish Terrier and the West Highland White Terrier – all seem to have a common ancestry. The Dandie Dinmont Terrier remains the odd one out, and his antecedents seem to be much more complex.

THE EARLY YEARS
There are records from Scotland, dating back to the 15th century, which describe dogs of low height with rough coats being used to chase foxes and other vermin. It is not, however, until the mid 1800s that we begin to find any mention of the colour of these dogs. Colour is very important in the West Highland White Terrier, as his colour is part of his name – which is rare in the world of pedigree dogs. The white referred to in the West Highland White Terrier is a true colour; it is not albinism (lack of colour pigment).

The Cairn Terrier played a part in the make-up of the West Highland White Terrier.

The history of the colour of the West Highland is very pertinent to the development of the breed. It seems from the accounts of many contemporary authors that, for many years, white and cream puppies were destroyed at birth, as it was thought that they were somehow inferior and weak when compared to their darker coloured siblings.

Given that the white or cream colour seems to appear frequently enough for the records to indicate their fate, it would seem that this colour is, indeed, one of the natural and possibly even dominant colours of these terriers. So we may construe that the breed is not, as some believe, an artificial man-made breed. It is true that selective breeding of this colour eventually took place, but it is fair to say that the modern West Highland, in all of his glory, can show a very long ancestry.

The light colour is also an important clue to the notion of a common ancestry among the terrier breeds of Scotland. Cairn Terriers can be a very light fawn colour, Scottish Terriers come in a very light wheaten colour, and cream Skye Terriers are common.

The history regarding the selection of white pups is interesting but not satisfactorily conclusive. Many of the early supporters of the breed recall that

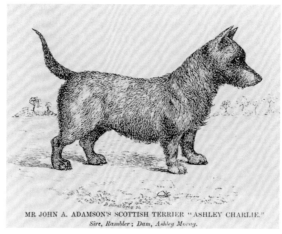

MR JOHN A. ADAMSON'S SCOTTISH TERRIER "ASHLEY CHARLIE."
Sire, *Rambler*; Dam, *Ashley Moray*.

Ashley Charlie, a Scottish Terrier, reproduced from Whinstone's *Dogs of Scotland*, published in 1891. The common ancestry between the Scottish breeds is easy to see.

they contacted kennels in Scotland, asking for "a good white puppy", only to be told that there might be a long wait, as interest in the whites was growing. What is not clear is the reason for this new interest. Many stories, some apocryphal, indicate that there was a recognition that white dogs were easier to see during the course of the hunt.

The most famous of these stories comes from Colonel Malcolm of Poltalloch, the man credited (wrongly) with the introduction of the breed. He tells of shooting a favourite red dog by mistake, and vowing henceforward to only keep white dogs. A very similar story comes from Captain Keane in England, while Captain Edwardes in Wales was developing the Sealyham Terrier for the same reason, using, it is said, West Highland Whites

in his breeding programme in order to reduce size and strengthen the colour.

Mrs Cameron Head (Inverailort) gives us an indication that white dogs had been kept by her family for many years, as her maternal grandmother, the daughter of 'The McLeod' (Head of the Clan McLeod) told how the white dogs were kept both for work and as family pets by both her father and her grandfather.

Given that Mrs Cameron Head's grandmother was born in 1800, this puts the keeping of white dogs back well before 1750.

This brings us to Colonel Malcolm of Poltalloch, who has been regarded by many as the developer of the breed. It is known, both from his own writings and from those of other authors, that he never laid claim to this honour. Indeed, the evidence seems to suggest that white dogs were still being put down at Poltalloch in the 1870s. The date of the shooting incident with the red dog is not known.

SHOW STATUS

At dog shows post 1890, we can see entries for a variety of terriers from Scotland, some of which were white. They were entered under many names, White Scottish Terriers, White West Highland Terriers, Roseneath

NAMING THE BREED

Colonel Malcolm of Poltalloch's real claim to fame is his involvement with the formation of the first breed club, set up in 1905. He organised the meeting in Glasgow when the first Breed Standard was drawn up. He was elected as president of the new club, and members tried to register the new breed club as The White West Highland Terrier Club. The Kennel Club agreed to the formation of the club, but insisted that the name of the breed be changed to The West Highland White Terrier. Within a very short time, a second club was formed, which became The West Highland White Terrier Club of England, and Colonel Malcolm became its vice president.

The Colonel resisted the idea that the breed should be known as The Poltalloch Terrier, as he knew it to be an old breed and not a new variety developed at Poltalloch.

The original 'Poltalloch Eleven' kept by Colonel Malcolm at his home in Poltalloch, Argyllshire.

West Highland White Terriers at the Inverailort kennels, owned by Mrs Cameron-Head (daughter of Head of Clan McLeod) pictured about 1909. The dogs have been identified by Mrs Cameron-Head as Shian, Roy, Speirrag and Sychar. They clearly indicate that a type existed at Inverailort in the very early years.

Early winners from the Inverailort kennels, pictured in 1911 with Mrs Cameron-Head.
The dogs are (left to right):
- Inverailort Dhoran: First-place winner in a puppy class at the LKA show in 1908. He was exported to America, and went on to win 14 firsts for his new owners.
- Inverailort Roy: Winner of two firsts at LKA, and two firsts and a Challenge Certificate at Birmingham.
- Inverailort Speirrag: Mother of Roy, and a big winner in her own right.
- Inverailort Sychar: A successful stud dog.

Terriers and even Poltalloch Terriers. Colonel Malcolm was a serious exhibitor of these dogs during this period, spanning to 1906, when the Kennel Club recognised the breed and it was included in the register of purebred dogs. After this date, Colonel Malcolm ceased to be an active exhibitor of dogs.

Many other people had begun to exhibit West Highlands during this period. Dr Flaxman (Pittenweem) exhibited and won well with his White Scottish Terriers, though he, too, curtailed his showing activities shortly after the breed became registered with the Kennel Club. There is written evidence from Colonel Malcolm, which indicates his dissatisfaction with the Breed Standard as drawn up by the two new clubs formed to promote the breed, and, possibly, Dr Flaxman also realised that his stock was now of the wrong type to win in the show ring.

The most successful breeder and exhibitor to come through the pre- and post-registration period was Provost Colin Young (Cairn) of Fort William. In 1907, he became the first breeder and owner of a Champion West Highland White Terrier – Ch. Morven – who was born on 28 March 1905. This male dog was three-quarters West Highland White Terrier and one-quarter Scottish Terrier through his maternal grandsire, Glenquoich. Colin Young was also the breeder of the first bitch to become a Champion, Ch. Cromar Snowflake, owned by the

EXPORTS TO THE USA

In the United States, the breed first appears as a show dog in 1906 under the name of the Roseneath Terrier, and in 1908 the American Kennel Club lists the breed in the Stud Book. The name of the breed was officially changed in 1909 to the West Highland White Terrier, and the UK Breed Standard was adopted virtually unchanged. The West Highland White Terrier Club of America was also formed and registered in 1909.

The first US Champion was an English import, sent out by Holland Buckley, the author of one of the early books on the breed (1911). The dog was registered in England as Clonmell Cream of the Skyes, but in the US he became Ch. Cream of the Skies. His antecedents seem to be unknown, giving rise to the probability that, like many early Champions, he came from unregistered stock.

Countess of Aberdeen.

At Crufts 1908, Colin Young swept the board, as Morven and Cromar Snowflake won the dog and bitch Challenge Certificates, and their son, Argyle, was Best Puppy. Morven and Snowflake won the Brace class and, when joined by Argyle, they walked away with the Team prize.

THE BREED DEVELOPS

Looking at the first 10 years of the breed in the UK, leading up to the curtailment of shows in 1917, Provost Young bred six Champions and accumulated a total of 41 Challenge Certificates. He was not active as an exhibitor after 1914, when the First World War started, probably because of his political commitments in Fort

William and his role as a farmer at a time of national crisis. He was president of The West Highland White Terrier Club from 1908 until his death in 1927.

Several dogs from the era before the First World War need a special mention. Champions Morova and Runag were the top-winning dog and bitch of this period, both winning 13 Challenge Certificates. Morven managed to gain 12 CCs and so just missed out on the record. Interestingly, Colonel Malcolm dismissed Morven without a prize card at one of his two judging appointments.

Ch. Chatty of Childwick won the most Challenge Certificates in any one year, with a grand total of eight in 1915. Ch. Kiltie, born in

Ch. Morven: The first Champion in the breed. Painting by F. T. Daws.

May 1907, gained his title in 1909 and was quickly exported to the United States for the princely sum of £400 – the equivalent of a small fortune in today's terms. Kiltie was followed across the Atlantic by Glenmhor Model and Dazzler Sands who both quickly gained their titles in their new land.

The breed experienced a rapid rise in popularity in the UK, as shown by the registration figures between 1907 and 1918. A total of 4,099 dogs were registered during this period with 1913 showing the highest annual figure of 631. A total of 29 dogs gained their title between 1907 and 1916.

THE IMPACT OF WAR

The First World War had a major impact on dog breeding, though the full effects of the difficulties did not materialise until late in the war. Food had been available for dogs and puppies, though it had not been easy to get. Then, in 1917, the government introduced a food ban, which prevented any domestic animal from being given food that a human or a food-producing animal could eat. This ban was strictly enforced.

In order to complement the government legislation, the Kennel Club introduced a ban on registrations, starting on 8 September 1917. A licence to breed was made available under special circumstances. The result was that many dogs and bitches were exported, particularly to the United States.

Dog shows were slow to get going after the war; the situation was worsened as a result of the severe influenza pandemic of 1918 and an outbreak of rabies in the same year.

One dog, White Don, was particularly affected by the breeding ban. He was born in October 1918, so he could not be shown. But he truly deserves his place in the breed history for his prowess as a sire and, more importantly, a dominant grandsire. He sired one Champion, four other CC winners, and 12 dogs who gained a Stud Book entry. However, as a grandsire he is on the pedigree of 25 Champions, often appearing on both sides of the pedigree.

THE WOLVEY WEST HIGHLAND WHITE TERRIERS

Some of the top pre-war kennels managed to come through these difficult years and went on to produce quality dogs. Perhaps the most famous of them all is May Pacey (Wolvey). She came from a wealthy family – her father owned Sketchley Dry Cleaners, a name that was, until recently, visible in every high street in the United Kingdom. Her interest in dogs began with Greyhounds, Whippets and Poodles, but after her marriage in 1910, she turned her attention to West Highland White Terriers.

She made up her first two Champions in 1916: Ch. Wolvey Piper and Ch. Wolvey Rhoda. Piper had been bred by Sam McLeod on the Isle of Skye, and so he was a true son of the West Highlands. Rhoda was spotted at eight weeks old in the window of a pet shop in Bond Street,

London, thus showing May's eye for a good dog. Both of these dogs were sent to the United States in the late years of the war. They had, however, been mated together to produce Wolvey Pedlar. Pedlar did not become a Champion, but he was the sire of the first owner-bred Wolvey Champion, Ch. Wolvey Jean, who gained her title in 1922.

In 1938, Wolvey Pattern gained his title and he, too, was exported to the United States because of the fear of impending war. He became the first West Highland White Terrier to go Best in Show at the Westminster Show 1942, held in Madison Square Gardens in New York, under his new name, Ch. Wolvey Pattern of Edgerstoune. The second West Highland to win this title was also an English-bred dog. He was Ch. Elfinbrook Simon, owned by Barbara Keenan, who took top honours in 1962. Several Wolvey dogs and bitches won Best in Show in the United Kingdom in the years between the wars.

Between 1916 and her death in 1963, Mrs Pacey made up 59 Champions and 14 other dogs had one or two Challenge Certificates. A total of 21 American Champions carried the Wolvey affix. This is a record unlikely ever to be beaten.

Mrs Pacey held every office in The West Highland White Terrier Club of England, and was its president for 23 years. She was responsible for maintaining the club through the two difficult war periods.

Although her major love was the West Highland Terrier, she

Ch. Wolvey Poacher, one of the many Champions owned by Mrs May Pacey, 1934.

had an encyclopaedic knowledge of all Breed Standards and was much in demand as an international judge of all breeds.

INTERBREEDING WITH CAIRN TERRIERS

The year 1917 was momentous in terms of the development of the West Highland White Terrier in the USA. Taking a lead role, the American Kennel Club introduced a ban on registering any West Highland White Terrier where a Cairn Terrier appeared in the first three generations of the pedigree. This edict is a clear indication of the practice of interbreeding, and highlights the common ancestry described earlier. Cairn Terriers had not been registered in the UK until 1910, and there was a debate at the time as to whether the Cairn was a shorthaired Skye Terrier or a separate breed in its own right.

In the UK the idea of a ban on interbreeding became an extremely contentious issue. The Kennel Club had sounded out breeders' opinions in 1916 but, perhaps due to the war, no action was taken. When, in 1924, the matter was again brought forward, breeders took very clear sides and a great debate took place in the dog press. Many very famous dogs of the period were cited as examples of why the practice of interbreeding should continue. Ch. Hyskear of Childwick (1915), Ch. Ornsay Sporran (1925) and Ch. Wolvey Fanny (1923) were examples of dogs with a close Cairn heritage.

The argument was finally settled on 8 November 1924 when the Kennel Club agreed that interbreeding between Cairn Terriers and West Highland Whites would not be allowed after 1 January 1925.

THE YEARS BETWEEN THE WARS

Mrs Pacey maintained that the breed came to its best during the inter-war years. Many kennels, famous on both sides of the Atlantic, made their debut between 1918 and 1939. Selecting a few for special mention:

* The Cooden kennel, owned by Mrs O. Williams, made up 10 UK Champions between 1926 and 1934. Six American Champions also carried the Cooden affix.

* The Rushmoor kennel, owned by Miss V. Smith-Wood, also had 10 Champions made up in the UK between 1928 and 1939. Ch. Ray of Rushmoor was exported to the United States, again to the Edgerstoune kennel, owned by Mrs J.G. Winant. He gained his American title, but became more famous as the sire of 10 Champions, nine of them carrying the Edgerstoune affix.

* The Furzefield kennel, owned by Mrs D.P. Allom, started up in this period. Mrs Allom bred or owned nine Champions between 1926 and 1959. However, she is better remembered as the owner of a very important stud dog, Furzefield Piper.

Piper was said to have lost a tooth in a kennel fight, so never gained a Stud Book entry in his own right; he did, however, go on to sire nine Champions. One of his sons, Ch. Hookwood Mentor, went on to sire seven Champions, including Ch. Barrister of Branston who, in turn, was the sire of 10 Champions.

* The Calluna kennel, owned by Audrey Wright, bred/owned eight Champions between 1931 and 1958.

* The Leal kennel, owned by Molly Turnbull, made up six Champions between 1929 and 1939.

* The Clint kennel, owned by Mrs Barbara Hewson, made up eight Champions between 1931 and 1937.

WORLD WAR TWO

World War Two had a very different impact on the dog scene from that of the 1914-1918 era. During the First World War, the only year without dog shows was 1918. In comparison, Harrogate Show was held on 3 September 1939, the day before the Second World War was declared – and this was the last dog show until 1946. There was no breeding ban, as in the first war, but food rationing caused breeders great problems.

Turning to the words of Mrs Pacey, she tells us that, "One was able to get some dog biscuits, and bread was not rationed. Horse meat was not easy, but we could get some every now and then. I learnt then that it was impossible to rear puppies without meat – nothing else can take its place. I had one lovely puppy. My ration, a few ounces of meat a week, was not nearly enough for him – but I could do without it."

Once again, many good dogs were sent abroad, particularly to the United States where they did very well for their new owners.

THE BREED POST-WORLD WAR II

Dog shows in the UK began again in 1946. These tended to be single breed club shows, as

ANALYSING REGISTRATIONS

A total of 154 Champions were made up in the 32-year period between 1907 and 1939. Compare this with the 121 Champions made up in the 12 years between 1947 and 1959, and it becomes obvious that the breed is really on the up. Registration figures for the same periods also indicate this upward trend: 18,923 dogs were registered between 1907 and 1946, and 15,087 between 1947 and 1959.

This trend continued throughout the 1960s when 31,471 dogs were registered in that decade – 98 dogs were awarded the title of Champion. The 1970s saw 111 Champions with registration figures of 37,940. There had been a change in the way in which the Kennel Club recorded registrations for a couple of years in the middle of the decade, which reduced the number of dogs registered; however, this did not detract from the obvious continuing upward trend.

The 1980s saw another change in the registration system, but not until 1989. From 1980 to 1988, 40,451 dogs were registered. In 1989 the Kennel Club insisted that all dogs in a litter be registered and named. This resulted in 15,604 registrations in that one year alone. There were 123 Champions in the 1980s.

The registration changes makes the figures for the 1990s seemingly go through the roof with 158,063 puppies born and registered. A total of 120 Champions gained their title.

Halfway through the first decade of the 21st century, registrations stand at the 50,000 mark, so there seems to be a slow down on the previous decade. This slow down has also been reflected in the number of exhibits entered in shows, which is roughly two-thirds of what it was in the late 1980s compared to the early 1990s era.

there was no benching available after the war. Only four pre-war Champion stud dogs appeared to be active in this immediate post-war period. They were: Ch. Melbourne Mathias (9 years old), Ch. Wolvey Prefect (12 years old), Ch. Leal Flurry (11 years old), and Ch. Leal Sterling (8 years old).

Two of these four dogs were to prove very important in terms of the continuity between the pre-war and post-war lines. They were Ch. Leal Flurry and Ch. Melbourne Matthias. Flurry was the sire of Matthias, and he also sired Ch. Shiningcliff Simon, who went on to sire six post-war Champions.

Ch. Melbourne Mathias was owned at the time by Mrs McKinney (Freshney). Mathias was the sire of Ch. Shiningcliff Sultan, Ch. Pygmalion of Patterscourt and perhaps most importantly, Ch. Freshney Fiametta.

Fiametta was the breed's first post-war Champion. She was born on 10 December 1943, and won her first Challenge Certificate in November 1946 at The West Highland White Terrier Club of England Championship Show. She gained her title in May 1947 at the East of England Ladies Kennel Society. Her fourth certificate came at The National Terrier Show under American judge Mrs J. Winant. However, her greatest day was yet to come when she won Best in Show at Cambridge. In total she won six CCs, all with Best of Breed. She was handled by the famous professional handler, Arthur Wade. Today, more than 60 years later, exhibitors look at her photograph and marvel at her type.

Melbourne Mathias was also the sire of a very useful dog named Freshney Andy. Andy was born in 1943 and won a CC in August 1946. Unfortunately, he died a month later but left as his legacy four Champions: Ch. Lorne Jock, Ch. Athos of Whitehills, Ch. Binnie of Branston, and Ch. Cruben Crystal.

Mathias was able to trace his lineage directly back to Ch. Morova (1913) and to a bitch called Cullaig, the dam of the first Champion, Ch. Morven.

The end of the war brought about many social changes and these changes affected dog showing. Prior to the war, the keeping and showing of dogs was very much the preserve of the wealthy middle and upper classes, who had room to house large kennels and could employ staff. They also had the finances and the time to travel around the country, showing their dogs in the days before mass car ownership and the motorway system, which has given easy access to shows.

THE BREED IN THE MODERN ERA

The West Highland White Terrier has held its own as a show dog throughout the second half of the 20th century. Some very strong kennels appeared early on after the Second World War, with many having a very long life, some continuing for more than 40 years. If we look at the top 10 kennels of all time in the UK

FAMECHECK

This internationally renowned kennel was owned by Miss Freda Cook. Between 1954 and 1997, a total of 38 Champions gained their title in the UK; 41 Famechecks gained American or Canadian titles, and 17 others were made up as Champions throughout the rest of the world. Miss Cook has not been active during the last 10 years.

(based upon the number of Champions bred or owned) then, with the exception of Mrs Pacey and her Wolvey kennel, all are post World War Two. Taking them in order, descending from the Wolvey kennel, they are:

ASHGATE

The Ashgate kennel was founded more than 35 years ago by Sue Thompson and her husband, Andrew, who died in 2004. Since 1976, there have been 35 Ashgate Champions in the UK, 24 in the USA and Canada, and 33 others around the world.

BRANSTON

Mr Brunel and Mrs Mary Dennis started their kennel just prior to the war, but activities were understandably curtailed by the hostilities. The First Branston Champion came along in 1948

and the last in 1973. Between those dates, 25 dogs gained their UK titles, and 10 became Champions in the USA. Mr Dennis served as chairman and president of The West Highland White Terrier Club of England. Mrs Dennis wrote a very comprehensive book on the breed.

LASARA

Barbara Graham comes in 5th place in the top 10 leading kennels. She began breeding in 1948, in partnership with her mother, Mrs Gladys Hazel. This duo made up four Champions between 1963 and 1973. Barbara then went into partnership with Jane Kabel. This partnership made up a further nine Champions until it too was dissolved in 1986 when Jane returned to Holland to start her own kennel, Llovall, which is once again in the UK. Barbara carried on alone and bred another 10 Champions. She died in 2005. In addition to 23 UK Champions, there were two Champions in the USA and 24 others, mostly in Scandinavia. Barbara served a term as president of The West Highland White Terrier Club of England.

BIRKFELL

Owned by Miss Sheila Cleland, this kennel is unusual in that it is made up mostly of bitches. A total of 19 Champions have come from this kennel, but only three are male. However, two of these males hold records in the breed. Ch. Birkfell Sea Squall won his

**A trio of Birkfell Champions: Ch. Birkfell Student Prince, Ch. Birkfell Samite and Ch. Birkfell Silver Slipper.
Photo: Anne Roslin-Williams.**

first Challenge Certificate when he was just six months old and gained his second while still a puppy. He is still the youngest dog to win a CC. At the other end of the spectrum, Ch. Birkfell Student Prince is the oldest dog to gain his title, which he did at the age of 11 years, 3 months. He was a grandson of Sea Squall. Sheila served the committee of The West Highland White Terrier Club of England as vice chair and president.

HAWESWALTON
Sue and Ken Hawes had a 15-year foray into the breed between 1981 and 1995. During this short period, 17 Champions were made up in the UK, 12 in the USA and two in Europe, making it the 7th placed kennel in the top ten list.

WHITEBRIAR, NEWTONGLEN, VALLANGE
In eighth place, there is a three-way tie (giving us our 10 kennels) between the Whitebriar kennel owned by Joyce Beer 1963-1987, the Newtonglen kennel owned by Mary and Adair Torbet (founded in 1972 and still going), and the Vallange kennel owned by Keith and Shane Harris (1995-2005). They all have 15 Champions to their credit.

The Newtonglen kennel has sent four Champions to the USA, while six USA Champions and 10 others around the world own the Vallange affix. After the death of Mrs Beer, her partner, Maureen Murphy, returned to her native New Zealand where many of her dogs have since gained their titles.

TOP HONOURS
Perhaps the greatest indicator of the strength of the breed during this modern period comes from the fact that West Highland White Terriers have twice won the ultimate accolade of Supreme Champion at Crufts dog show.

The first of these special wins came in 1976 when Ch. Dianthus Buttons took the top spot, handled by Geoff Corish, who went on to become a top professional handler following this victory.

Some 14 years later, Ch. Olac Moonpilot took his place on the rostrum as Supreme Champion. He was handled throughout his career by his breeder/owner Derek Tattersall. Moonpilot is also the top-winning West Highland with a total of 48 Challenge Certificates to his

Ch. Olac Moonpilot: Crufts Best in Show 1990, pictured with one of his sons and the BIS trophy.

credit. During his career, he won the Terrier Group 18 times and was Best in Show at General Championship Shows 10 times.

He took the record from Jeanette Herbert's Ch. Glenalwyne Sonny Boy, who amassed a total of 33 CCs, nine Groups, and was three times Best in Show. He was handled to his wins by the professional handler, Ernie Sharpe.

The breed's all-time top stud dog is Ch. Ashgate Sinclair, who has sired 19 Champions. His nearest rival is Ch. Haweswalton Houdini, the sire of 12 Champions, with Ch. Famecheck Hallmark coming a close third with 11 Champion offspring.

Bitches get much less opportunity to produce Champions, but the records show that two bitches have each produced five Champions – they are Ch. Wolvey Peach and Ch. Famecheck Lucky Mascot. Four bitches have each produced four Champions. They are: Binny of Rushmoor, Wolvey Popinjay, Waideshouse Wickedness, and Ashgate Bleaval of Fernforest.

CENTENARY CELEBRATIONS

In 2006, the breed celebrated its centenary in real style with three special events taking place. The first, in April of that year, was the Centenary Championship Show of The West Highland White Terrier Club of England. The Best in Show was Pepabby Priceless, who later became a Champion.

In June 2006, a Joint Centenary Show was held with The West Highland White Terrier Club at Dumfries where Best in Show was Dwilencia Dream Lover

Ch. Krisma Streetwise: This dog took top honours at the Centenary Championship Show.

at Rozamie, also later a Champion.

The final event in the centenary celebrations was held in January 2007 when the Dog of the Year Show was held, appropriately near Wolvey, where Mrs Pacey's started her kennel. Top-winning dogs and puppies were invited to compete under a panel of three judges whose names were kept secret until the event. The judges were: Geoff Corish (Sealaw), Ela Berry (Incherill) and Ferelith Somerfield (Oudenarde). The event was a great success and looks likely to be repeated in future years. The winning dog was Ch. Krisma Streetwise, owned by Mrs Dot Britten.

In the first 100 years of the breed, 810 Champions have gained their title. Anyone looking at pictures of the breed as it has progressed over the past 100 years will note that although there are changes in presentation, the breed is still recognisable as the small, white, hardy terrier he was developed to be. His character has endeared him to millions, and he is internationally known as a popular family pet. His ability to hold on to this character, whatever else might change, assures his future.

A WESTIE FOR YOUR LIFESTYLE

Chapter 3

Once you have decided that a West Highland White Terrier is your chosen breed, the next stage is to consider whether owning a Westie would suit your way of life, and, equally, whether your way life would suit a Westie. Owning a dog is a big commitment and not something to be entered into without a great deal of thought and consideration. Westies can live long lives – I currently have one that is approaching 17 years – so your commitment has to be long term.

Many of us today live busier lives and do more travelling than our parents and grandparents. Owning a dog years ago would have been less complicated, because wives and mothers would probably have been at home during the day. In general, life would have been less frantic, with less traffic on the roads and fewer holiday breaks in the course of the year, let alone frequent trips abroad. It was easier to accommodate a dog into the household. Today, there are few homes that have someone at home all day during the week. The question then arises as to how you can own a dog as a pet without compromising his welfare.

TAKING ON A WESTIE

Firstly, you have to understand that the Westie is a busy, sociable little dog and the idea of leaving him alone for long hours during the day would be totally unacceptable. A Westie needs company and stimulation and, of course, exercise. It is mostly these characteristics that have made the West Highland White Terrier such a popular breed.

One of the breed's main attributes is its size. The Westie is a small dog, and is easily transportable. How many times have you seen a Westie travelling happily in the back of the car as part of the family (a Westie wouldn't consider himself anything less)? I have come across many families where the husband would like a large dog, but there is limited space available. However, once the man of the family meets a Westie, he falls in love with his outgoing personality, robust nature and sturdy body. The Westie is small in size, but big in personality, and so, in many ways, he is an ideal dog, fitting more easily into modern life than many of the larger dog breeds. A Westie

You need to find a litter of healthy, well-bred, typical Westies.

The breeder will help you to find the right puppy to suit your lifestyle.

wants nothing more than to be integrated into a busy family life and to take part in family outings – being left behind is not part of their vocabulary.

When you are looking to purchase a Westie, a reputable breeder will question you as to whether there is someone at home during the day. If the answer is negative, they will probably not let you have one of their

puppies. It would be cruel to take a puppy away from his littermates and the familiarity of his surroundings, and place it in a home that is deserted all day. A puppy would feel completely abandoned. Therefore, a good breeder will ask if there is someone at home and will not entertain a puppy that they have bred and nurtured being left for long periods of time.

Some owners are lucky and

can organise their work schedules so that different members of the family are at home to cover the week. If this is not possible, there are other options that may provide a solution. Over recent years, businesses have mushroomed that offer pet sitting, doggie day care, and dog walking services. These are often small, one-man bands and are advertised at the local veterinary practice

The Westie is small in stature but he still needs regular exercise.

and in local newspapers. A dog sitter will come to your home and spend some time with the dog, taking him for walks, feeding him and giving fresh drinking water. At doggie day care, your dog will be cared for, along with other dogs, on a daily basis.

Clearly, dog sitters will differ in quality, and it would be necessary to meet the person who would be helping with your pet to be sure that you

trust them for their reliability and level of care. You should also ask for references from others who use their services. Properly organised, this situation can work very well and prevent your dog being left for hours on end. This does not mean that you should disappear for five days a week for long hours, as the dog will still have far too much time on his own – and when you return from work,

you will probably be too tired to take the dog for a walk or give him attention.

Unless you are going to have a family member at home during the day, you should not even think about having a small puppy that needs frequent and consistent attention if he is to be house-trained and well adjusted, and also bond with his new owner. Care and time spent training and socialising a young puppy

FINANCIAL COMMITMENT

It is also important to weigh up the financial implications of owning a dog. Obviously, you need to find the purchase price of a Westie puppy, and the feeding costs, but you also need to budget for vaccinations and vet fees should your dog become ill. Treatment of a pet dog can be expensive. It is worth considering taking out pet insurance that will cover your dog if he becomes ill or has an accident. There are many pet insurance schemes, and you will need to compare some of them to find the right one for you.

Another cost that should be considered is whether you will need to pay to have your pet looked after if you go away or are ill. You may be very lucky and have a relative or neighbour that will be happy to look after your Westie for you, but many make the offer and then back out when it becomes a reality. It is a good idea to look around and ask other dog owners about boarding kennels in your area. Word soon gets around if an establishment is good, and also if it is poor. When you have done some asking around, go and see a couple of kennels and get a feel for the standard of care and cleanliness. Another option is to use a house-sitting service. This is not cheap, but it does give your home some protection at the same time by not being left empty. Again, you will need to be sure of the agency you use and take references and guarantees of the person who is to live in your home.

makes a huge difference to the type of dog he will become. I am not advocating that a puppy should be kept in the owner's company 24 hours a day. Puppies should get used to spending some time alone – not for long periods, but certainly for the odd half hour and hour. A puppy who cannot be left alone and feel secure will grow into an adult that frets and possibly causes damage when he finds himself alone. A happy dog is not one that is desperate if he finds himself alone. Sometimes, without thinking about the future, an owner will be too protective and anxious with a

puppy, and then cannot understand why he grows into an adult that is over dependent on human company and becomes a burden rather than a companion.

A SUITABLE HOME

What about the amount of space needed by a Westie? Ideally, you should have a house with a garden that your dog can run round in without escaping. One of the assets of the Westie's smaller stature is that he can be kept in a house with a small garden, providing that he is taken for regular walks. Just remember that the

Westie is a master at finding a little hole where he might escape. You will need to check that fencing is secure, with no gaps that an inquisitive West Highland will use as an exit route. Remember, too, that Westies are terriers and therefore great diggers. You can train a Westie to a degree not to be destructive, but if your priority is a pristine garden, then maybe you need to consider whether this is the dog for you.

A Westie may be small, but he is not a lap dog. There are those that manage to keep a Westie in a flat, with no access to a garden, but this is

Do your homework in order to find a responsible breeder that produces quality puppies.

no easy feat. Great dedication is needed to make sure that the dog gets sufficient exercise. You need to be prepared to rise and go out early for the dog to relieve himself, and then take him out regularly during the day. Again, this would not be easy at all with a puppy, who would prove difficult to house-train if he cannot be popped outside at frequent intervals. Few breeders would be happy to let a puppy go to this environment.

FINDING A BREEDER

A responsible breeder will ask you a lot of questions. A breeder puts a lot of effort and love into breeding and rearing their puppies, and will not want them to end up in unsuitable homes. I would be very wary of a breeder who had puppies readily available and asked no questions of you. Finding a reputable breeder is most important if you want to end up with a healthy and happy Westie.

Sadly, West Highland White Terriers were one of the most exploited breeds in puppy farms some years ago. Their numbers exploded, and many poor specimens were bred purely for commercial reasons. Commercial and disreputable breeders still exist, but they have learnt to be cleverer at disguising what they are up to. Beware of breeders who have lots of different breeds for sale. And I would also be suspicious of a breeder who keeps young puppies in a barn or an outbuilding where they cannot be properly socialised.

You will need also to check that the litter has been registered with the Kennel Club. Do not be taken in by breeders who offer you cheaper puppies if they are not registered.

The best plan is to contact one of the major breed clubs

in the UK, which keep lists of breeders with litters, or litters that are expected. These breeders will be club members, and will have a genuine interest in the breed. A lot of these breeders will also show their Westies. I can hear you saying that you don't want a show dog, but this is not the point. Good show dogs are few and far between in litters, but what you will get from this type of breeder is someone who has extensive knowledge of the breed, and who will have used good bloodlines to produce quality puppies. Once the breeder has chosen what puppies they

are keeping from a litter as show or breeding prospects, they will sell the remaining litter members as pets, making sure they go to permanent, loving homes. Good breeders will also give you support with information and advice throughout the lifetime of your dog.

Puppies that have been well socialised and acclimatised in the breeder's home will settle more easily in their new homes. When rearing a litter, I make sure the puppies have experienced the sound of the vacuum cleaner and the washing machine etc. Their pen is positioned in the house

so that they see and hear everything that goes on and that they meet all our visitors. I make sure they have been in different locations, including running on grass and being outside to have some exercise.

There are some pet owners who decide to have a litter from their pet Westie; they often make a very good job of rearing the litter and thoroughly enjoy the experience. This may be a good source for a puppy, but remember that you will, hopefully, have your Westie for a long time, and you should therefore be prepared to wait for the right one. An

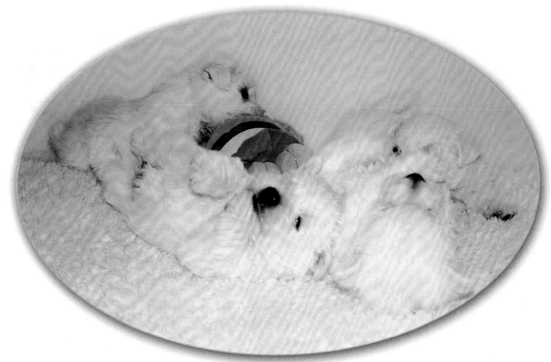

Westie puppies are irresistible, but do not let your heart rule your head when assessing a litter.

impulse buy from the wrong kind of breeder – because you cannot bear waiting – may well be a mistake that you regret for a long time.

Regardless of how you locate a breeder with puppies, the final decision as to whether you buy from them has to be yours. If you feel unsure or uneasy with the set up, trust your instincts and do not buy a puppy. Many disreputable breeders are kept in business because people feel sorry for the puppies they go to see. If you harden your heart and refuse to buy a puppy from an unreliable source, it will help to put an end to this type of backyard breeding.

ASSESSING THE PUPPIES

There are a few guidelines to consider when looking at a litter of puppies that will help you recognise if they have been well cared for and well reared.

- The puppies should feel well rounded and firm.
- Check that the ears are clean. Well-kept puppies should not have canker (ear wax) in the ears.
- The eyes should be bright and alert, with no sign of weeping or discharge.
- The nose should be black and shiny, and there should be no discharge here either.
- The area around the anus should not be stained, as this could indicate that the puppy has had diarrhoea.
- Although your puppy should look well nourished, he should not have a large, rounded, distended tummy. This would be a sign that the puppy has worms, which will compromise his health. The breeder should have regularly wormed the puppies and have a record of this.
- When you pick up a puppy, he may struggle at first, but

The puppies should be kept in a clean, hygienic environment.

You will want to see the mother with her puppies, as this will give you some idea of the temperament they are likely to inherit.

he should feel vigorous, certainly not thin and floppy or limp.

- Once the puppy has been stroked and reassured, he should relax. A puppy that has not been sufficiently handled by the breeder and not been in contact with people will show signs of panic and fright; he may feel rigid and perhaps make a terrified scream at being handled by a human. Westies are outgoing and

love meeting people once they have been introduced. Therefore, a fearful puppy would be a concern for the future.

- It is essential to see the mother with her puppies. Her attitude and personality will give you an idea of what your puppy will become. Ideally, you want to see a bitch who is friendly with visitors and playful with her pups. She may not look at her best

after nursing a litter, as she may have lost a little weight, and hormones can affect the coat. However, this would not stop her from looking clean and healthy.

- Do not presume that every litter has a runt in its midst. On the whole, Westies do not have large litters and if the puppies have been properly reared, there is rarely a weak, unviable one. If one or two of the pups

Watch the puppies playing together and you will see their individual personalities emerge.

are a little smaller, but are lively and healthy, there is nothing to worry about.

THE RIGHT CHOICE

Before you make a decision, I suggest that you ask yourself the following question: "If I bred a litter, would I keep them in this condition?" If the answer is no, then don't buy. Good breeders will always be happy to answer your questions. They will want to meet you before they agree to

let you have one of their puppies.

It is important to make it clear what you are looking for in a Westie. Is he to be a loving companion for one person, or will he live with a noisy, active family? Just like humans, some puppies are leaders and some are followers; some are very active, others rather laid back. A good breeder will advise you of the differences between the puppies, and will help

you to choose a puppy that is most likely to suit your family and your lifestyle. For example, a more excitable puppy is probably not the best choice for a family with younger children. In this situation a pup could become hyperactive, egged on by the youngsters in the family who are noisy and excited. In a family that consists of adults and older teenagers, this puppy would more readily learn his place and grow up to

PUPPY COATS

Westie puppy coats differ greatly, and a first-time owner may need a little guidance:

- **Smooth and sleek:** This type of coat will probably grow into a harsh coat and be easy to keep clean and groom. However, it takes time to grow in length, and may make the puppy look plain for a while.
- **Long and profuse:** There are puppy coats that have more length and will be more profuse. This coat will also grow into a harsh coat once it is stripped and trimmed.
- **Soft and profuse:** Occasionally you come across a coat that is not typical of the breed; this is a very profuse, soft coat that resembles a Persian cat. Of course, these puppies can appear very attractive, and if the dog is not to be shown, then it is not going to be of great importance. However, this type of coat will need more careful grooming, as it will tangle more easily. Some coats of this type prove difficult to hand-strip and will require clipping.

be a respectful and well-behaved dog.

Depending on the size of the litter and whether or not you are one of the first prospective buyers, you may be offered some choice, but I would strongly urge you to take advice from the breeder.

MALE OR FEMALE?

One question often asked by prospective owners is whether there is a difference between having a male or a female. This really is down to personal preference. Many first-time owners have the idea that a bitch will be more affectionate. This is not true; I have found that males bond very loyally with their owners and family. Bitches also will be loving companions, possibly being rather maternal as they mature, although this is not always the case. Whether your puppy is male or female is probably less important than what individual temperaments and characteristics are within the litter.

If you choose a bitch puppy, you will have to cope with her coming into season every six months unless you have her spayed. If you buy a male puppy, you may decide to have him neutered if he is not to be used for breeding, though this is rarely necessary.

A SHOW PUPPY

What if you want to buy a Westie to show as well as being a pet? The first step is to acquaint yourself thoroughly with what this means. Learn what the Breed Standard requires of a show dog. Go to breed club shows where you will meet other exhibitors and breeders, and watch the Westies in the ring. Don't rush to buy a Westie straight away. It is a good idea to apply for membership to a West Highland breed club where you will get to know about shows and seminars and the various activities they organise.

There is more to being an exhibitor than walking around the ring with a dog. Learn by reading and watching at shows, and find out what you should be looking for in a good specimen. Take into account that there is a lot of coat trimming and preparation before a Westie is put into the show ring, so you need to look at how the dogs are presented and shown. It may look easy watching the experienced exhibitor, but it is a craft that has to be learnt.

Choosing a male (left) or a female (right) comes down to personal preference.

The breeder will 'stand' a puppy so that you can see if he has show potential.

In some cases, a puppy will have a health check before leaving the breeder's home.

If, after this, you still want to go ahead, approach an exhibitor/breeder whose dogs you admire. It is likely that you will have to wait some time for a puppy, and even then remember it is a pet with promise, not a fashion accessory that comes with a warranty. So much can go wrong as a Westie grows from puppyhood to adulthood. The second teeth may not have the correct scissor bite, the body may not grow on in the way the breeder had hoped, or the dog may not have the temperament to want to show in the ring. However, you have to start somewhere and for those of us who enjoy showing, it is an intoxicating hobby.

Most breeders/exhibitors will tell you that the best time to choose a show puppy is at about eight weeks. At this age he should be well balanced, presenting a square shape. His neck should flow into his shoulders, like a champagne bottle not a beer bottle. His tail should be held erect. His head should show a broad skull and ears, not hanging to the side. Most importantly, he should have 'attitude'.

HEALTH CHECKS
The puppies should have started a worming programme, and you will also need to find out whether they have received any inoculations. If you buy your puppy before he is 12 weeks old, which is quite possible, he may not have received any vaccinations.

Some pedigree breeds have specific health checks required by the Kennel Club to screen problems inherited

WRITTEN CONTRACT

Good breeders will often have a written contract that they will ask you to read and sign. If this is so, you will need to read it carefully to consider all the points and be sure you are happy to sign it. A typical contract will include the following:

- The puppy should be taken to your vet within seven days of purchase, and if the vet finds something wrong with the puppy, then the breeder will refund your purchase price and take the puppy back into their care.

- In the case of a puppy being returned, a specific time limit will be stipulated.
- Some breeders also put restrictions on the Kennel Club registration papers. These restrictions may designate that you may not breed from the puppy in the future; if you were to do so, the Kennel Club would not register the progeny. Another restriction may be that you do not export the puppy. In order for these restrictions to be implemented, the breeder must explain them to you and you will have to agree to them in writing or in a contract of sale.

in that particular breed. However, there are no specific checks that the Kennel Club requires for Westies.

Some breeders have puppies checked by a vet before they are sold. In any event, it is advisable to have your puppy health-checked by your own vet when you take him home. If there is a problem, most responsible breeders will take the puppy back straight away. Make sure you know the breeder's policy on this point before you purchase a puppy.

TAKING ON AN OLDER DOG

What about those whose lifestyle and work commitments will not allow

them to have a puppy, but they still have dreams of owning a Westie? In this situation, the answer would be to take on an older dog. Sometimes a breeder may have a bitch that has had a litter or two and is ready to retire from breeding duties and now needs a new home as a loving family pet. Alternatively, a show breeder may have kept a puppy with a view to showing him, but he has not come up to the exacting standards of the show ring. In this case, the dog needs a pet home.

But even if you are taking on an older dog, you still need to be realistic about your work schedule. No dog should be left for great lengths

of time, but an adult dog will tolerate a certain amount of time on his own. Be honest in your assessment: if you cannot give a dog sufficient time and company, then wait until you can.

If you think you can cope with an older dog, you can contact breed clubs that will put you in touch with breeders who have older dogs available – although you may have to wait.

Taking on a puppy is very demanding, but giving a home to an older Westie is not always an easy option. An adult dog will have got used to his life and home, and will need time to adjust to his new surroundings. You will also need to know whether the

It may suit your lifestyle to take on an adult dog.

dog has been house-trained, because some dogs may have lived in a kennel environment and may not, initially, respect your fitted carpets. Fortunately, most adult Westies can be house-trained very quickly. Most Westies want to please their owners and, with encouragement, will quickly get the message.

It is important that when you first take on an older dog, you allocate a period of time to be with him so you can get used to each other. It would be unthinkable to take on a Westie one day and then leave him on his own the very next day. Try to coincide your holiday dates with the arrival of the dog. Again, full-time work is incompatible with owning a dog.

RESCUED DOGS

Another way of owning a Westie is to go to Westie rescue or an all-breed rescue organisation. Although the desire to give a dog a good home is very laudable, you need to be aware of what you are taking on. A Westie is in rescue for a reason, although this is often through no fault of his own. In some cases the previous owner may have had to give up the dog because of a change in personal circumstances, such as ill health or divorce. The previous owner may have made a good job of caring for and training their Westie, but this is not always the case and a rescued dog's behaviour may be less than desirable.

The Westie Rescue Society does put a lot of work into assessing the dogs that come

**This is a breed that
will steal your heart.**

into its care. Efforts are made
to find out if the dog has any
difficult behavioural issues that
need understanding, care, and
training to rectify. These
problems are often the result
of bad treatment by the
original owner – perhaps the
dog has been handled in a
heavy-handed manner or been
pulled around by young
children. Sometimes a Westie
is neglected because the
original owner has bought the
dog on a whim and then
realised what was involved in
caring for a dog.

Most of these dogs will have
come from commercial
breeders who have not made
the effort to check that their

puppies are going to suitable
homes. This type of breeder
will probably have bred
without sufficient care and may
have been indiscriminate in
their choice of breeding stock.

Some rescued dogs have
ongoing health issues that will
need addressing; the rescue
society will give advice after
the dog has been checked and
treated by a vet. However,
some will have health
problems that will need
watching carefully, maybe
throughout their lives.
Whatever the reason for the
dog being in rescue, you need
to be prepared to put a lot of
love, care and patience into
his rehoming. This is not an

easy or a cheap option to
owning a Westie.

It can be very rewarding and
satisfying to gain the love and
trust of a rescued dog, and to
help him overcome any
problems. But be under no
illusion that this is an easy
ride. But those dogs that are
successfully adopted are a
credit to their new owners and
bring them years of pleasure.

HEART STEALER
All in all, a lot has to be
considered when you decide
to incorporate a Westie into
your family. However, for
those willing to make the
commitment, this is a breed
that steals your heart.

THE NEW ARRIVAL

While you are eagerly awaiting the arrival of your West Highland White Terrier, it is a good idea to check your house and garden to make sure you are providing a safe and secure environment.

IN THE HOME

If you are taking on a puppy, you will have to be doubly careful, as a small pup will get up to all kinds of mischief as he investigates his new home. Look for gaps where he can get trapped, such as behind the fridge or washing machine, and make sure all electrical wires are out of reach. A bucket of water could pose a real danger if a puppy climbed in and couldn't get out, and bottles with toxic substances are potentially deadly. View your house as if you were letting a baby crawl about in it, but then think about the fact that the puppy is a lot smaller and has very sharp teeth. Pups don't see danger, so you need to see it for them.

A Westie pup may also try to get on to higher surfaces, such as chairs and sofas. It is one thing getting up – but it is all too easy to fall. In one of our recent litters we had a puppy staying a bit longer. He quickly worked out that he could heave himself on a little chest from which he would then be able to get on our settee. My worry was that if he wanted to jump off the settee, he would not use the chest but would leap from a height and hurt himself. We therefore had to remove the chest. Although a puppy has supple bones, which may not break as easily as in an older animal, a fall can still be disastrous. An injury to a hip joint, for example, could result in long-term lameness.

Stairs can be equally hazardous, so it is advisable to fit a baby-gate to prevent access. A baby-gate can also be used if you want to prevent access to particular rooms in the house.

If you are taking on an older dog, he is unlikely to get into trouble in the same way as a puppy, but he will feel very unsettled until he gets used to his new home. The priority is to make your Westie feel secure, and to keep the atmosphere as calm and quiet as possible until he finds his feet.

IN THE GARDEN

Make sure the garden is dog-proof and the fence is secure so a nosey pup cannot find a way out. A fence needs to be at least 90 cm (3 ft) high, and tough enough so it cannot be chewed. You will also need to check that gates are secure and kept shut at

The inquisitive Westie will explore every corner of your garden.

dangerous, as the pup can go in, or even fall in, and perhaps not be able to get out. If you have a garden shed, make sure it is secure. Substances such as slug killer and anti-freeze are highly toxic, but plant feeds or other animal feeds could also cause problems.

BUYING EQUIPMENT

You do not need to buy a lot of equipment for a Westie – unless you want to – but there are a few essential items for the shopping list:

INDOOR CRATE

A crate is an invaluable item of equipment for a puppy – and an adult will also be happy to settle in a crate lined with cosy bedding. A crate can be bought from a pet shop in different forms and sizes. A collapsible crate is ideal, as you can use it for travel, when staying with friends and family, and even in hotels. We recommend a crate that is 55 cm deep, 45 cm wide and about 50 cm high (22 x 18 x 20 inches approximately). It may seem big for a small puppy, but I can assure you that the pup will grow up fast and the crate will still be large enough for an adult dog. See Crate training, page 60.

BEDDING

In the crate you need to put some bedding. I recommend using machine-washable synthetic fleece, but, of course, an old blanket or towel will do. The amount of bedding you buy depends on how often you wish

all times. A Westie loves to dig and a small puppy can slip through holes you may not even be able to see easily.

Check the garden for poisonous plants – you can find the necessary information on the internet or by going to a library.

You will be amazed how many plants are poisonous; some are more toxic than others, but quite a few can make a Westie sick, and a puppy will be more severely affected. Some plants can also cause skin irritations.

A garden pond can be

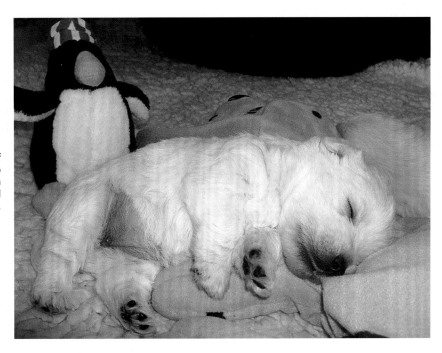

Puppies need a lot of sleep, so you will need to locate a bed or a crate in a place where your pup will not be disturbed.

to use the washing machine. Fleece bedding usually dries quickly, but you will need at least two pieces so you can change the bedding when necessary. Clean bedding encourages the pup to stay clean. Once it is soiled, the pup won't hesitate to make it dirty again.

BED

Your Westie will appreciate a bed in addition to his crate for daytime use. There is a wide variety of beds available, but remember that a puppy loves to chew, so foam bedding should be avoided. Wicker baskets are not ideal for pups for the same reason. Hard plastic beds are best, as they can be easily

cleaned. Of course, the crate can be used as a bed, but you may prefer to let the pup have a bed as well, which can be moved easily to wherever you want it to be.

FEEDING BOWLS

Your Westie will need two bowls: a feeding bowl and a water bowl. There is a wide range of bowls to choose from. I recommend stainless steel bowls, which are easy to clean and are virtually indestructible.

EXERCISE PEN

Known as an X pen, this is a playpen for your Westie. A readymade X pen usually consists of four or more wire panels hinged together. It is also

possible to create your pen by buying some panels (meant for making compost heaps) at a garden centre and securing them with cable ties. The advantage of an X pen is that it provides a safe place for a puppy, but the pup can still see you and feel part of the family. A puppy needs plenty of sleep, just like a baby, and he can rest in his crate after having a play session with his toys. (See A Special Place, page 59)

TOYS

The top priority is to find safe toys – but remember that an adult's requirements are different to that of a pup. Puppy teeth are sharp but not as strong as adult teeth. Pups love soft toys that

Westies love to play, but make sure the toys you choose are 100 per cent safe.

make a noise when they play with them. Some older Westies are fine with soft toys, but some can be very destructive. Westies usually love playing ball; some will play fetch and some just love to run around after a football, usually barking loudly!

For young puppies we have found some baby toys are ideal, either soft ones with a rattle or hard teething rings. We always cut off anything that sticks out too much, such as labels, to help make the toy last longer. It is important to be aware that a swallowed squeak can cause a lot of internal damage, so these toys should only be allowed when you can supervise. This is even more important where an adult is

concerned, as he is more likely to rip up a toy. One of my old-time favourites, known as Fun, lost his life at 11 as a result of swallowing part of a rubber toy, so you can never be too careful.

BONES

A puppy will enjoy chewing on rawhide bones, but adults can have a tendency to swallow bits, which can get lodged. We give our Westies sterilised bones or strong Nylabones, which seem to last a lifetime. The bigger the bone, the safer it is.

COLLAR AND LEAD

For a puppy you need a small, soft collar with a lead. An adult will need a stronger, adjustable

collar, as adult Westies do differ in size; he will also need a stronger lead. With both the collar and the lead, make sure the fastenings are sturdy, as you don't want them to snap when you are walking near a busy road.

Extending leads can be useful, as long as they are used with care. A dog should not be walked on an extending lead on the pavement, where he could dive out into the traffic. An extending lead is best used in an area where there is enough space for a dog to run around, but it is not safe enough to let him off the lead.

Never leave a collar on a dog if he is not supervised. Dogs have

THE IMPORTANCE OF ID

Some breeders microchip or tattoo their puppies before they go to their new homes. If this is not the case, you will need to decide what form of ID you want for your Westie. In all situations, a Westie should wear an identity tag, attached to his collar, giving contact details. But you may wish to consider a permanent form of ID. Microchipping is now common practice, and you can ask your vet to perform this simple procedure.

You may opt for a permanent form of ID in addition to a disc attached to the collar.

been known to strangle themselves as a result of getting a foot stuck in a collar, or catching it on something.

GROOMING GEAR

A good starting point is to ask your puppy's breeder to show you what grooming tools they use, and seek advice as to what you should buy. Equipment is the same as for an adult, although you may prefer to use a smaller brush at first. A soft baby brush can be handy for a pup to get used to being

brushed, but it won't be effective enough to keep knots out of the coat. It is very important to get your pup used to being brushed and combed. Almost from the first day you take your pup into your house, you need to get him used to being brushed and handled all over. The younger you start, the better.

FINDING A VET

Talk to dog owners in your area and find out about the local practices. A vet who really cares for small animals is so

important. You will also need to find out what facilities are available at the practice and what arrangements are in place for emergency cover. Some of the bigger practices provide their own cover, while others may use back-up from other local practices. Bear in mind that just because a practice is big, it doesn't mean it has a good reputation. My advice is to shop around and find a practice that seems most likely to cater for your West Highland White Terrier's needs.

At last the time has come to collect your puppy.

COLLECTING YOUR PUPPY

So now you are all set for your new dog's arrival. After all the planning and waiting, the big day has arrived and it is time to collect your puppy. In all the excitement, make sure you have the correct paperwork from the breeder. This will include:

• A pedigree (three generations or more)
• A contract of sale
• A worming record
• A diet sheet

If you are getting an older dog,

you will be given Kennel Club registration documents, but this is not always the case with a puppy. Some of us, especially those of us who show our Westies, prefer to register the pups when they are a little older. In this situation, you will be sent the registration at a later date. The breeder should explain this to you when you collect your puppy.

In some cases, a puppy may have received his first vaccination before leaving the breeder, in which case you will need a record of this. However,

do not think the breeder is uncaring if no inoculations are given. Some of us, depending on the age of the pup, prefer to wait until the puppy is older. All too often a new owner's vet will repeat the same inoculations, and we feel the puppy will be over-inoculated. Some also feel that a pup should not be inoculated too young and too often.

If you have met the breeder and viewed the litter some time in advance of collecting your puppy, you may have had a chance to get a supply of the

Arriving in a new home can be a daunting experience.

food the breeder has been using. But most breeders will give you some food to last a few days. It is very important not to change food at this early stage. If you change the pup's food straightaway, it will be too much for the pup to cope with on top of the change of home, and may well result in digestive upset. This applies to an older dog too, of course.

TRAVELLING HOME
Make sure the new pup or adult is safe in the car while you travel home. If you have to go on your own, be sure to have a crate for the dog to travel in. Bring a water bowl, and an empty bottle that you can ask the breeder to fill with water. This will only be necessary if you have to travel some distance.

If it is a hot day and you don't have air conditioning in your car, take some extra old towels and dampen them with cold water so the dog can cool off by lying on it. This is a useful tip to bear in mind for future journeys during the summer months. Frozen water bottles can also come in handy if you wrap them in a towel for the dog to lie against. A cool bag is recommended to keep drinking water cool. My Westies won't drink lukewarm water or dirty water, for that matter.

If you stop en route, find a safe and quiet place and be sure the dog cannot slip out of his collar. Remember, you are still a stranger to your West Highland White Terrier; he will not necessarily respond to your voice and may well panic and run away. There are far too many dogs who have got lost in this

A child and a West Highland can be the best of friends, but interactions should always be supervised.

way. If you are travelling with a puppy, he is unlikely to be lead and collar trained, so it is safer to put some newspaper in the crate so the puppy can relieve himself if need be.

ARRIVING HOME
Resist the temptation of inviting your neighbours or all the children's friends to meet the new dog on his first day. Let him settle in peace. It will be overwhelming for a puppy or an adult dog to come into a new home, and it will not help if he has to meet lots of new faces as well. It is important for the dog to meet his own new people and learn who his new housemates

are before meeting other friends as well.

INTRODUCING THE FAMILY
If you have children, encourage them to be as calm and as quiet as possible. Ask them to sit on the floor, so the puppy can meet them as he chooses. Let the puppy come to the child, not vice versa. A puppy could feel threatened when approached by a child. A puppy is not a toy for the children, but, with proper guidance, he will become their friend. A puppy needs to sleep a lot and should not be disturbed by children when he is resting. Do not allow the children to pick up the pup and carry him about.

A puppy can be very wriggly, and accidents happen all too easily.

A young pup is used to exploring the world with his mouth: biting, chewing and mouthing. When he comes to his new home, the puppy must learn that this sort of behaviour is not acceptable if it is applied to people – especially children. Do not encourage, or even tolerate, a pup that bites or mouths hands, fingers and other human body parts. This should not be allowed, even in play. A dog pup I bred had a habit of pulling on the children's socks and sleeves just for fun, and it turned out that the children

An older dog will accept a new puppy as long as he still feels that he has a special place in your family.

played tug-of-war with the pup. The puppy could not see the difference between the toy and the socks or sleeves. I told the family to stop the children playing tug-of-war and let them play ball instead. Most Westies naturally retrieve, and running after the ball is good exercise for the dog and the child.

If a pup bites because he does not want to be groomed, or just out of playfulness, respond by saying "No" very sternly and then ignore him for a few seconds until he calms down. You can also try making a sudden noise, for example shaking a tin filled with little stones, which may startle the puppy into stopping his undesirable behaviour.

MEETING THE RESIDENT DOG
If you already have a dog, the first introduction should be handled sensitively. The present dog will see the house and garden as his property and may be inclined to guard it. The new puppy doesn't know this is going to be his new home and may be insecure about it. It is a good idea to let the two dogs meet outside the house, both on a lead. Monitor how they respond to each other; if they appear calm and settled, you can take both into the house.

If you have a puppy, allow the resident dog to come up and sniff him while he is sitting on your lap. Some dogs get used to each other quicker than others, so it is a matter of reading the older dog's body language and responding accordingly. At first let the dogs sniff each other, and try not to interfere as they get to know each other. However, do not leave them alone together until you are completely confident that the resident dog has accepted the newcomer. Once the pup can go out for a walk in the big wide world, you can take them on joint outings and they will enjoy each other's company.

thing you want. Cats can usually escape to a higher surface – just make sure that they are never driven into a corner. With smaller pets, great care should be taken. It may be possible for them all to live in peace, but it takes careful handling.

HOUSE TRAINING

For a pup, I advise that a part of the garden is set aside for potty training. The reason for this is two-fold: the puppy learns that this is the area where he goes to relieve himself and does not get distracted, and it is easier to clean up after your puppy.

You will need to take your puppy out at the following times:

- First thing in the morning
- After a meal
- When the pup wakes up after a nap during the day
- After a play session
- Last thing at night.

In between these times, watch for signs of your puppy becoming restless, which may indicate that he needs to be taken out. A puppy will need to relieve himself at least every two hours, so a watchful eye is needed at all times. Some pups will indicate that they need to go by heading towards the door – but, to begin with, you will probably have to do the 'thinking' for your puppy.

Every time you take your West Highland White pup to the potty area, use a command that needs to be the same every time, for example: "Wee wee", or

Introductions to other pets should be made gradually, keeping the situation as calm and quiet as possible.

Always make sure the resident dog gets at least as much – if not more – attention than the new arrival. It is very much like introducing a new baby to the older children.

OTHER PETS

All other animals that live in the house should be introduced gradually, preferably one at a time so you can observe their response to each other. Make sure both animals feel safe and secure, and are not threatened by the other. If another animal, such as a cat, guinea pig or rabbit, is likely to run away, it might stir the chasing instinct in your new Westie – and that is the last

If you are vigilant and take your pup out at regular intervals, he will soon learn to be clean in the house.

"Quickly". You may think it sounds daft, but the puppy will quickly learn to associate the word with the action, and this will help with the whole process of house training. As soon as the pup has relieved himself, give him lots of praise. Go over the top so your puppy knows that he is a star. Try to make your voice sound really exciting – maybe using a higher pitch – so your puppy knows you are especially pleased.

If you have an adult dog, treat him like a puppy, taking him out to the potty area to begin with, so that he learns what is required. Remember to clean up after your dog – and always go equipped with plastic bags if you are taking your dog out to public places.

A SPECIAL PLACE

I strongly advise all new puppy owners to create an area in the house that is to become the pup's own space. This is where the X pen comes into its own. The best place to site the pen is on a tiled floor, or if this is not possible, buy a small piece of vinyl and put the pen on it. Place a small indestructible bed in the pen, a water bowl, and some toys. It is also a good idea to line the front part of the pen with newspaper. Obviously, you still need to observe the pup and let him outside regularly, but if he has an accident, it is easy to clean up.

There are a number of advantages to using an X pen:

- A house is full of potential hazards, and an unsupervised puppy will get into mischief. This may be harmful to himself, and your house and possessions are also likely to suffer.
- House training is much easier when you can observe your puppy and take him out when required.
- A puppy is safe and secure in an X pen, particularly at times when you have visitors and doors may be left open.

CRATE TRAINING

A crate can be placed within the X pen instead of using a bed. If the crate door is left open, the puppy will learn to go in and out as he pleases. I always recommend that a puppy sleeps in a crate at night so you are confident that he is safe and secure.

To begin with, a puppy may object to being confined in a crate, but he will quickly learn to see it as his own safe haven. If your puppy is reluctant to use his crate, give him his meals inside it and he will soon build up a good association with it.

I advise some fun playtime before retiring for the night, as it will make the pup sleepy and more likely to settle down for the night. Then let him out into the garden, and put him in the crate with a little treat. I always say "Goodnight" to my Westies; they do learn to associate certain words with certain times and actions. Most dogs are very clever – and Westies certainly are.

A puppy learns through play and therefore needs mental stimulation.

When a puppy comes into your home, the golden rule is to start as you mean to go on.

At first the pup may object to being confined, but he will soon begin to like his home. Do not give into your Westie's protests, or you will end up with a dog that demands attention all the time. A puppy that learns his boundaries will grow into an easy-going adult.

I am not saying the pup is never allowed to have a run outside his pen, but this should be only at times when he can be supervised by an adult.

The amount of time a pups needs to spend in the pen varies. A very lively pup that runs around a lot will have to be persuaded to go for a sleep. Another pup will find a quiet place and go to sleep by himself,

but pick the puppy up anyway and put him in the pen. As soon as the pup wakes up, take him outside, as he will need to relieve himself. As the pup grows, he can spend longer periods of time outside the pen, as long as he is watched closely.

Right from the first day your West Highland White Terrier enters your house, you should not allow behaviour that you won't tolerate later on. It may seem cute when a puppy is swinging from the curtains or chewing the furniture, but this type of behaviour is far from amusing when the Westie is an adult. Once you allow certain behaviour, it becomes a habit that is difficult to break.

MEALTIMES

A Westie will need four meals a day when he arrives in his new home. It is best to stick to the breeder's routine for feeding, if possible, as this will help the puppy to settle. You can always change the schedule over a period of time to one that suits you better. Like babies, puppies – and older dogs – thrive on routine. I think it gives them a sense of security. For more information on feeding, see Chapter Five.

EARLY LESSONS

If you are taking on an adult Westie, he will probably be lead trained, but if you have a puppy, you will have to get him

HANDLING

An important first lesson is to accustom your puppy to being handled.

Pick up each paw in turn.

Check the ears.

Part the lips so you can examine the teeth and gums.

accustomed to wearing a collar and walking on the lead. Some puppies seem to rebel against a collar and lead more than others, and it takes a bit of patience to overcome a stubborn streak.

Start by putting on a soft collar and see how the pup responds. Some will scratch and roll around to try to get it off, but, if you are lucky, your Westie will not take any notice. I knew of two Scottish Terrier pups that would just sit in a corner – not moving, and refusing to eat – until their collars were removed. I have not had this experience with a Westie, but the best plan is to take things slowly, allowing the puppy to get used to the collar for short periods of time. Do not proceed to attaching a lead until the puppy has accepted the collar.

Your Westie will also need to learn some basic obedience, such as Sit, Stay and Come (see Chapter Six). Start straight away, as it is so important that a Westie does not rule the house and family. Train with kindness and give many rewards. Call your pup by the name, and reward big time when he comes to you. Give vocal praise, a cuddle and a little snack. Let it all be fun, but at the same time make sure the dog knows you are the boss. Be gentle, but also be firm and consistent.

Take the pup to as many new places as possible as soon as he is fully covered by his inoculations. When a puppy is young, he takes matters in his stride and will grow up to be calm and confident in all situations. At the same time, teach your pup that he has to stay at home on his own for periods of times (not hours on end, though). At first, just leave the room where the pup is, and, if he is OK with that, step up the amount of time you can leave him, graduating to leaving him for short periods when you are out of the house. This is a very important lesson, as you don't want a Westie that can never be left on his own and suffers from separation anxiety.

SUMMING UP

It is vitally important to give a dog the correct upbringing – with lots of love but also with firmness. Your Westie is a pack animal and it is very important for the dog to know who is the leader of the pack. This has to be you, as it needs to be an adult and one that deals with the dog most of the time. Do not expect children to be able to train a pup, as the pup is more than likely to see the children as his equals.

A well-brought-up Westie gives so much pleasure – much more than a dog with no manners at all. Westies are clever and can learn a great deal as long as they are treated well and consistently. But they can also learn bad habits easily – and once those are established, it is very difficult to go back in time. What you imprint at a young age is there forever.

Work hard at rearing and training your Westie and you will have a companion that is second to none.

If you put in the work when your puppy is young, you will be rewarded with a well-behaved companion.

THE BEST OF CARE

Chapter 5

So you have just taken a West Highland White Terrier into your home! Well, what a pleasant few years you are going to have with this big-hearted, lovable, clever, witty, happy, eager to please, big dog in a little body. But do remember that he will be quick in everything he does. People sometimes say to me: "Oh, terriers snap." They do not – or should not – "snap", but it is important to remember that the Westie was bred to catch vermin, and a dog cannot do this if he is slow. Typically, a Westie has quick, sharp jaw movements, which you will see when he is catching a ball or picking up a toy in play. A terrier is the very opposite of a soft-mouthed retriever, who is bred to collect fallen game; a terrier is bred to be as fast and as agile as the game he is pursuing.

You can make generalisations about the West Highland White Terrier, but each one is an individual, and people who have owned a number of Westies always remark on this. A West Highland has 'personality plus'; he loves to be with you, go where you go, and do what you do. He is content to stay on his own for a while, but he gives such a welcome when you come back, it is as though you have been away for weeks!

Feed him well (but do not overfeed and get him fat), exercise him, love him, and he will, in return, give you many years of companionship and unquestioning devotion.

UNDERSTANDING NUTRITION

All nutrients are important to health; they interact with each other and work together to keep your dog happy and healthy. Nutrients don't work alone: they work in harmony with each other within the body. Raw food is a great source of natural nutrients with superior bioavailability, i.e. amino acids and protein, enzymes, antioxidants, vitamins A, C, D, E, K, B1, B2, B5, B6, and B12, biotin, choline, folic acid, fatty acids, phosphorus, magnesium, iron, potassium, copper sodium, zinc, calcium.

PROTEINS
These contribute most to structural growth and can be found in meat, fish, eggs and cheese.

FATS
These are obtained through raw chicken, meat, and bonemarrow, which has the omega 6 group of essential fatty acids.

CARBOHYDRATES
These are found in cereals, good-quality wholemeal dog biscuits,

The West Highland White Terrier is an active dog that needs a good-quality, well-balanced diet.

bread and oats, and fruit and vegetables. Carbohydrates are important for energy as well as brain and nervous system function.

VITAMINS

- Vitamin A – for bones, hair, immune and respiratory systems, skin, soft tissue, and teeth. It also helps to fight infection. Vitamin A can be found in alfalfa, cod-liver oil, eggs, fruit, fish, kelp, meat, meaty bones, and vegetables.
- Vitamin B complex – for cells, eyes, gastrointestinal tract, hair, liver, nervous system, mouth and skin. It can be found in the same foods as for vitamin A, plus in nuts and seeds.

- Vitamin C – for adrenal glands, blood, bones, capillary walls, cells, connective tissue, heart, mucous membranes, nervous system and teeth. It is found in alfalfa, fruit, kelp, meat, meaty bones, and vegetables.
- Vitamin D – for all aspects of growth. Lack of Vitamin D can be a major factor in the production of an unhealthy skeletal system. It is found in alfalfa, cod-liver oil, eggs, fish, meat, meaty bones plus sunlight.
- Vitamin E – for arteries, lungs, skin, and the circulatory, heart, nervous and glandular systems. It is important for breeding animals, aiding

fertility in the dog, and it assists in the prevention of abortion of foetuses.
- Vitamin K – for correct clotting of the blood, bones, liver, and the gastrointestinal system. Trace elements can be found in a balanced diet and will be added to processed dog food, either canned or dry.

MINERALS

These are needed for reproduction and growth. The most important is zinc for the full and proper development of the nervous system.

Don't forget another essential – love – which the dog gets from us!

FEEDING GUIDELINES

Feeding the West Highland is straightforward if you have an understanding of a dog's basic needs. A dog is a carnivore, and in the wild he would catch and eat his food raw. Obviously, our dogs are now domesticated, but a terrier still has strong animal instincts, which you will see if he spies a running rabbit, rat or mouse or even a cat! I once had an infestation of mice in a chicken food store. I let in a West Highland bitch, who caught dozens of mice within minutes, using the special 'snap-flick' movement. She was in her element – and we never had problems with mice again. But I could not keep her away from the store, as she was always on the look out for more mice to catch.

A Westie is not suited to a rich or overly fatty diet. Feeding this type of diet often leads to skin irritations, and tummy and bowel upsets, which will need treatment from a vet. Aim to keep the diet fairly plain, and if your dog is thriving on what you are feeding him, there is no need to make changes. You can turn your West Highland into a fussy eater by offering him lots of choices, and this will have a poor effect on his mental and physical wellbeing.

When you get your puppy home, he may not eat four meals a day, or he may leave food. Do not worry about this – it is simply because he has lost the competition from his littermates. Some puppies are also reluctant

To begin with, a puppy may miss the competition of feeding with his littermates.

to eat when they are first settling into a new home. If your puppy seems particularly hungry at breakfast or at any of his other mealtimes, increase the amount you feed at this mealtime so you can be confident the puppy is getting all the food he requires.

CHOOSING A DIET

How, when, and what to feed your puppy/dog can be a minefield, as there are so many types of food to choose from. Diets range from off-the-shelf food – canned, dried and pouched – to a natural, homemade diet. To begin with, keep to what the breeder has

been feeding, and if you want to change the diet, do so gradually, introducing new foods a little at a time over the course of a few days.

CANNED FOOD

There are many canned meats on the market; your job is to find a type that suits your dog.

Firstly, do not be swayed by advertising – just because it has your breed on the label, it does not necessarily mean that it is suitable for your dog. Read the breakdown of contents listed on the can and see what percentages of protein, carbohydrate and additives it has. An adult dog

Read the label carefully before choosing canned food.

A complete diet is manufactured for different life stages.

There is increasing interest in providing a more natural diet.

should not need a food with more than 8 per cent protein, just over 8 per cent for a puppy, and 7 per cent for the senior dog. Most canned food has a high rate of water in it (some as much as 75 per cent), some have a high rate of fat, and some have a high rate of soya. If you wish to use a canned food, do it by trial and error, finding out what suits your dog, especially his bodily functions, what suits his palate, and lastly what suits your pocket.

Beware of the quantities recommended by the manufacturers or you will be in danger of over-feeding. A third of a can is sufficient for an adult West Highland. Most manufacturers recommend that canned meat should be fed with a biscuit or mixer (not a complete food, which looks like a biscuit). Vegetables can also be added.

Once the can has been opened, keep it refrigerated and covered and use within three days.

POUCHED FOOD

Pouched foods are similar to the can, but very often contain more water and salt. The meat content is often chunky, with a lot of gravy or jelly. Again, it is important to check the protein content.

Once opened, the pouch must be refrigerated and treated as a canned product. Use sparingly, and see how your dog does on this product.

COMPLETE DIETS

Dry foods – or complete diets, as they are often called nowadays – are clearly labelled for puppy, adult or senior. Again, beware of the amounts recommended by the manufacturer and use your discretion! You must always have fresh water available when feeding this type of food: shortly after feeding, a dog will drink quite a lot, as the food absorbs fluid from his body. This type of food is convenient, it does not need

refrigeration, it can be left down all the time for choice eating, but it is oh so boring...

NATURAL FEEDING

Many dog owners are now turning to natural feeding advocated by Dr Ian Billinghurst in his books *Give Your Dog a Bone*, and *Grow Your Pups with Bones*. The diet he recommends is known as the BARF programme, which stands for 'biologically appropriate raw food'. I am a strong advocate of this method of feeding, as I like to feed what the dog would most eat naturally. This includes raw chicken and tripe with vegetables (which can be purchased ready packaged frozen at most good pet stores) and a little wholemeal biscuit or breadcrumbs. As the dog matures I gradually progress to feeding raw chicken carcasses or wings; backs and necks from turkey/duck is excellent if you can get a good, fresh source, but definitely do *not* give cooked

PUPPY MENU (BARF PRINCIPLES)

7.30am
Cereal (such as Weetabix, porridge oats or Ready Brek) with goat's milk.

11am
2 oz (57g) raw minced chicken/tripe/rabbit/lamb/beef with a teaspoon of minced mixed vegetables (see below). Baked beans can be used for vegetables, and two or three times a week a teaspoon of brown rice or pasta can be added. A small amount of puppy biscuit or breadcrumbs also can be used.

2pm
Milky drink fortified with either baby rice or Farex (no sugar or salt variety).

5.30pm
Raw chicken wing (I beat these with a hammer to begin with, to break the joint bones and snip the skin until the puppy gets the hang of what to do. Watch your puppy until he has finished the wing for the first few meals.

10.30pm
As the 7.30am meal.

As the puppy grows, you can cut out the milky feeds and increase the meat meals. By about four months of age your puppy should be on three meals a day, and then by six months he should have two meals per day. This will then be the pattern for life unless a medical condition changes this.

The following items can be added to the 11am or 5.30pm meal:

* Whitebait: raw and cut up with scissors and mixed with one meal per day (buy a few and freeze individually).
* Raw offal (i.e. heart or kidney): My dogs do not like raw liver, but you can try it, as every puppy is different.
* Organic live natural yoghurt: a teaspoonful per day mixed with any feed or just off the spoon. This does not have to be every week, perhaps every other week.
* Vitamins: alfalfa and kelp is given every other day on one meal per day. This is in powder form and is easily available.
* Omega 3 oil: this can be with cod liver oil. Be careful with this and do not give too much or too often; twice a week is sufficient, and only half a teaspoonful when an adult. An alternative is a salmon-oil capsule, which should be given two or three times a week. Flax oil can be given instead of cod-liver oil; it is very rich and too much will make a dog scratch and become over heated.

RECIPE FOR MIXED VEGETABLES
Put vegetables in a food processor; this can be any type of vegetable except potatoes or onions, and not a lot of peas, green beans or sweetcorn. The mixture must include some fruit; I use apples and pears, as my dogs do not seem to like oranges, but you can use any fruit you have available. To this add a garlic clove, some parsley and a raw egg (plus shell, if it is free range; otherwise, just the egg). Whiz all this together and freeze in small amounts to use as required.

SAMPLE PUPPY MENU

This is the diet sheet I give to puppy buyers who want to feed a more conventional diet, but it retains elements of a natural diet. I have given approximate mealtimes and quantities for a puppy aged eight weeks.

7.30am
Cereal (Weetabix or porridge) made with goat's milk (not cow's milk, as this seems to upset their bowels).

11am
2oz (57g) raw minced meat (tripe, chicken, turkey, beef or lamb) with a little soaked wholemeal biscuit or wholemeal breadcrumbs. Pasta or rice can be added instead of biscuit or breadcrumbs for a change, as can vegetables.

Vitamin supplements can be added to this meal (see below).

2pm
Milky drink fortified with baby rice or Farex. Alternatively, scrambled egg or rice pudding.

5pm
2 oz (57g) minced meat (cooked or raw) added to puppy meal, scalded with broth/stock minus the vitamin supplements.

10.30pm
As the 7.30am meal.

Note: When cooking minced meat, add water – but no seasoning.

---

bones, as these become brittle when cooked.

I have adapted a diet that has the BARF principles, but is more convenient for everyday use.

WATER
Fresh drinking water should be available at all times, but make sure your puppy does not just drink it because it is 'there' – or paddle in it, as one of mine does! I tend to offer water at regular intervals until the puppy is a little older and I can leave the bowl down all the time.

TREATS
Never feed your dog at the table, as he will soon get used to this

and become a nuisance, begging for food every time you sit down for a meal. If you want to give your dog treats, do so when you have finished your meal.

Do not give your Westie sugar, salt, chocolate, biscuits or cake – no matter how much he pleads. Fruit is fine to give as a treat if your dog will eat it. My dogs love apple, pear and, would you believe it, pineapple. Do not give dried fruit or grapes.

DANGERS OF OBESITY
Do watch your dog's weight, especially if he or she has been neutered. The correct weight for a West Highland White Terrier is around 16-18 lbs (7.25-8 kgs).

FEEDING REGIMES
I think that the mealtimes in a dog's life should be something to look forward to, although there are dogs with built-in clocks who know the time before you do, and will not rest until they have been fed. The option is to vary feeding times to keep your dog guessing when his dinner will be served.

With dry foods, a lot of owners leave the food down all the time and let the dogs help themselves, making sure fresh drinking water is always available. Personally, I do not agree with this method, as I believe it is unhygienic, with a strong danger of the food becoming contaminated by flies. However, how you feed your dog

It is your job to keep your West Highland White Terrier at the correct weight.

is a matter of personal choice, depending on what suits your dog and what fits in with your lifestyle.

SUMMING UP

To conclude on the type of food to feed your Westie, just remember what I said at the beginning – a dog is a carnivore and raw meat, bones and skin is what his body and intestines are meant to digest. This is my personal opinion, but do give some time and thought to choosing a suitable diet, and keep a close check on your West Highland White Terrier so that you

are confident that he is thriving on the diet you have chosen.

PLAY AND EXERCISE

Before bringing your puppy home, do make sure that your garden or yard is safe, as a West Highland is an accomplished escape artist and will find any gap in the fencing and dig his way to freedom…

All dogs need exercise, even when they are still small. It must be remembered that a puppy is still vulnerable while he is growing, so build up the exercise gradually. A young puppy can play

outside in a safe area as much as possible, weather permitting, as fresh air is very important.

Work on lead training in the garden (see Chapter Six) and by the time your puppy has completed his inoculations and your vet is happy that he can now mix with other dogs, he will be ready to be taken on short walks. Take him out among people and traffic, which will give him new sights and sounds to grow accustomed to. Gradually increase his walks until he is about nine to ten months old.

EXERCISING A WESTIE

If you give your West Highland a variety of exercise, he will enjoy life to the full.

To begin with, a puppy will get as much exercise as he needs from playing in the garden.

Westies love to dig, and, given the opportunity, will use up a lot of energy in this pursuit.

Never underestimate the speed of a Westie at full throttle.

Playing a game will exercise a Westie both mentally and physically.

If you can take your Westie on holiday it's a great bonus – he will love the opportunity to explore new places and be part of the family fun.

The adult dog is very adaptable in terms of exercise requirements. He will be able to go as far as you want, or he will be content to stay in the garden if needs be. However, free walking and running, under supervision, is what a Westie likes best. Owning a West Highland White Terrier – or being owned by a West Highland White Terrier – is a pleasure, and exercising is as much a benefit to you as it is to your dog.

Games with toys help a dog to develop physically and mentally. The West Highland White Terrier is a very intelligent breed, so he needs to be stimulated. Running to catch a ball is great exercise, as long as you are in a safe environment and your dog will come back to you! Watch the speed he goes when chasing a fast-moving object, such as a ball, just as if he were after the vermin he was bred to catch – it is magic.

Road walking is good for hardening muscle and keeping the toenails in trim. Take your dog on different routes so he does not get bored with the sameness of his walk. A lot of West Highlands like swimming, although my dogs will not even paddle in the sea – they run back as the water flows in over their paws! However, if your Westie is a swimmer, do be careful and

Your puppy will develop a double coat, which consists of a soft undercoat and a harsh topcoat.

make sure there are no undercurrents in the river, stream or sea, and check that there is a safe place where your Westie can get out of the water.

A country ramble is just what a West Highland White Terrier likes – with you, of course, in tow. He will have great fun sniffing out the rabbits and discovering new, exciting scents, but he will keep looking back, just to see you are still there. After a long country walk, my dogs return home and then twitch and yip in their sleep. I like to think they are dreaming of what they might have found – and given chase to!

GROUMING

Apart from feeding and exercising your Westie, he will also need regular grooming and trimming.

The weekly grooming you can do yourself; if you are reluctant to trim your Westie, you will need to find a good grooming shop/parlour who will do this for you on a regular basis. However, you must still keep your West Highland brushed out and free from knots and tangles. There is nothing more frustrating for a professional groomer than to have to cut out lumps of a dog's coat because it is so badly matted as a result of neglect by the owner.

I have often had dogs come in for grooming that I know have not had a brush through their coat since the last time I trimmed them. The owner may claim to have brushed the dog, but you can tell the coat has only been brushed down his back, and not been touched underneath or on the front or back legs. It is little wonder that a dog who has not been properly groomed ends up in a real mess, and also smells, especially if he is a male.

There is also the problem of the owner who uses incorrect grooming tools. The coat looks fine on the top but is matted underneath because the grooming tool has been the wrong type for the breed.

If you follow these guidelines on grooming your West Highland, you should have no problems and your dog will be a credit to you.

PUPPY GROOMING

Grooming should start at an early age so that the puppy is calm and relaxed.

Initially, a puppy needs to get used to the feel of the brush on his coat.

If nails are trimmed regularly, a puppy will learn to accept the procedure.

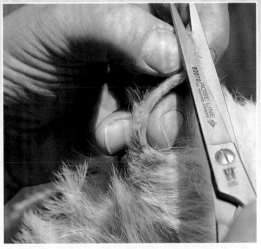

The hair on the ears is trimmed to give the correct shape, and to assist with the desired erect ear carriage.

JUNIOR GROOMING

If you have a pet Westie, you will need to continue grooming until the first trip to the grooming parlour. The undercoat can be groomed out, but the dead topcoat needs to be stripped out, using finger and thumb.

The dead coat is stripped out using finger and thumb. Powdered chalk is used to get a good grip on the hair.

The groomer moves round to the front. This puppy is now used to being on a grooming table, attached to a noose.

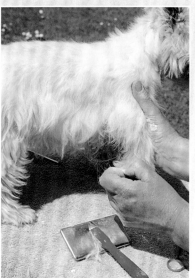

The groomer may work on the coat for just a few minutes a day so that the youngster does not become restless.

The coat will also need to be trimmed to enhance the shape, and to remove hair in the more sensitive areas. Here thinning scissors are being used to trim the tail and the hindquarters.

ADULT GROOMING

HAND-STRIPPING

The advantage of hand-stripping, as opposed to clipping, is that when the coat grows back, it retains the harsh texture that is typical of the West Highland White Terrier.

An adult Westie in need of a make-over.

The hair is stripped from the top of the neck.

Continue down to the shoulder, making a smooth transition from neck to shoulder.

The body coat needs to be stripped, working along the length of the back.

The coat on the sides should be stripped, but it should be longer than the hair along the back.

The coat on the undercarriage should be kept relatively long.

Go to the front of the dog and strip out the straggly hairs on the chest.

The hair needs to be stripped from the front legs – both in front and behind.

The back legs and the hindquarters need attention.

The long hair on the tail should be pulled out.

The coat on the head grows profusely, so hand-stripping is needed to get the correct shape and to remove the long hair around the eyes.

TRIMMING

It takes many years to perfect the art of hand-stripping and trimming a Westie. The aim is to enhance the dog's natural lines, but to retain the natural look that is characteristic of a terrier.

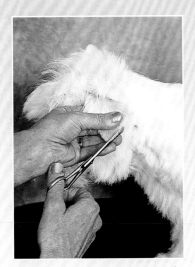

The edges of the ears are trimmed.

Thinning scissors are used to remove enough hair to reveal the eyes.

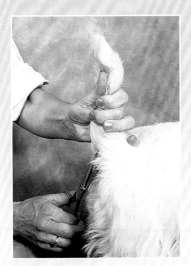

The hindquarters are trimmed moving up the tail, which should resemble a carrot, tapering to a point.

The hair along the line of the undercarriage is made level.

The back legs are shaped.

The hair is scissored around the back feet.

The hair that grows between the pads needs to be trimmed back.

GROOMING GUIDELINES

Start grooming your puppy as soon as you get him home. Lift him on to a table or bench, making sure he is standing on a non-slip surface, such as a rubber mat or a piece of old carpet. It is easier for you to groom the puppy off the floor, as this is his 'play' area where he is in charge, whereas on the table you are in charge. Your puppy will also get used to being off the floor when he has to visit the veterinary surgeon or grooming parlour.

As the puppy grows older and stronger, you can put him in a collar and attach a lead that has been secured to an overhead shelf or to the ceiling. This will keep your puppy in place on the table, and will give you two hands for the grooming session. A word of warning here: do not leave your dog in this position unattended, even for a second, otherwise the collar and lead could become a hangman's noose.

Start by using a medium-soft brush just to get your puppy used to it, and then use a slicker brush or a terrier pad. You will then need to comb through the coat.

I cannot stress how important it is to use the correct tools for the job. If you groom with the wrong brush, such as a long-pinned or bristle brush, it could mean that the old undercoat is not removed. When the dog gets wet, the undercoat then gets matted and can irritate the skin and make your dog scratch himself or, worse, nibble a sore patch.

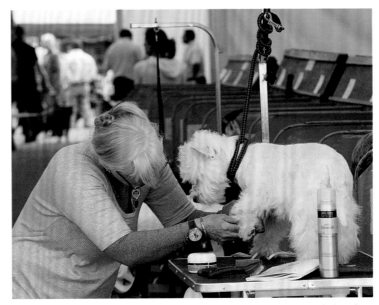

Presenting a Westie for the show ring is an ongoing process – including last-minute preparations.

When you start grooming your puppy, at about eight weeks old, there will not be much coat to brush, but it helps the puppy to be handled and off the floor, so he will be happy and relaxed by the time he is ready for his first trim.

As the adult coat grows, you will need to spend more time brushing and combing the coat. If the coat gets tangled, combing will be painful, so it is best to prevent this situation arising. Attention has to be paid to the hair under the armpits, thighs and around the feet where the hair is liable to get matted. If the dog is groomed regularly, it takes only minutes to do this thoroughly. The correct procedure is for the comb to go through the coat down to the skin, and not to skim through the top hair. The head furnishings should be combed forward over the face, and the leg hair combed down. A good grooming session will help to remove dead hair, scurf and dirt, and will also stimulate the blood circulation, which helps to prevent skin trouble.

Your puppy should have, or will develop, a double coat. West Highlands do not moult; the undercoat can be brushed out but the old top dead coat needs to be removed. This needs to be done about twice a year; in the case of bitches, usually after her season. Hand-stripping out the top coat is easy when it is about two inches (5 cm) long. The hair

A West Highland White Terrier beautifully presented and ready for the show ring.

can be plucked out with finger and thumb preferably, but there are many trimming knives on the market, which make the job easier.

PET HAND-STRIPPING

The correct way to keep your West Highland White Terrier in trim is to hand-strip the old dead coat out to allow new growth to appear. The show dog is trimmed all the time, which is an ongoing job, but you can keep the pet dog reasonably tidy by doing this two or three times a year yourself. Alternatively, you can take your dog to a professional groomer who specialises in hand-stripping.

STEP-BY-STEP GUIDE

- Groom your dog thoroughly, and then rub loose or block chalk into the coat, which will help you grip the hair. You can alternatively use rubber finger-stalls or a household rubber glove. These also help you grip the coat and protect your nails and fingers from the hair.

- Start behind the ears and at the top of the neck where the head joins the body. Keep the skin taut and pull a few hairs at a time. If you come across long, straggly hairs, take a strong grip and pull them out firmly.
- Work your way down the neck and back towards the tail, pulling the hair the way it grows.
- Go back to the neck and work your way down the sides of the neck; this is taken closer than the body hair.

- Leave the front leg hair longer, but do take out the long straggly hairs at the back and front of the legs. The front leg should resemble a 'pillar' after trimming around the feet with straight scissors.
- The coat on the sides of the dog is also left longer than the top of the back. You need to blend this in and down to form what is commonly known as the 'skirt', which can be as long or as short as you prefer.
- Work your way down the back legs towards the feet, pulling out the longer hairs and leaving room for new hair to grow. Again, the hair can be as long or as short as you want. Finish by trimming around the feet with scissors.
- The chest area and rear end are trimmed with thinning scissors, as these are very sensitive areas and pulling hair here can hurt your dog.
- The tail should resemble an inverted carrot, wide at the root and tapering to the point. You can trim the hair on the back of the tail with thinning scissors if your dog will not let you pluck out the hair. Trim around the anus with straight scissors to keep him clean.
- The head needs special attention. I always start by trimming the points of the ears (checking that they are clean and free from odour). I then brush the head hair upwards so I can see the long hairs standing up. Pull these out, and only leave hair at about two inches (5 cm) long on the

Nails should be trimmed on a regular basis.

top of the head.
- Work your way down each side of the skull, leaving the hair about three inches (7 cm) long, including the hair on the side of the muzzle.
- To round the head off, use thinning or straight scissors, or a combination of both. Hold the dog's head under the chin, and cut around the head, tapering up to the ears on each side of the head to gain the full chrysanthemum look. Let the dog shake, and then you will see if there are any straggling hairs left to pull out or tip off with scissors.

TEETH

Teeth need to be cleaned regularly, using a proprietary paste and brush, which are readily available in pet stores. You can also buy chewing aids for keeping the teeth and gums in

good condition, to be used after the second teeth come through, which is around six months. Do check that all the puppy teeth have dropped out; sometimes the puppy top incisors can get lodged between the descending new teeth.

As your Westie gets older, check that tartar has not built up on the teeth. If there is an accumulation of tartar, the teeth will need to be scaled by a vet. This will usually involve an anaesthetic.

EARS

Check your Westie's ears during his grooming session for any odour. You will also know that there is a problem if he cries when you touch his ears, if the ear drops, or if he rubs the side of his head. If you observe any of these symptoms, please consult your veterinary surgeon. I cannot stress this too strongly. You can buy proprietary ear washes, which are quite good for general cleaning, but they are not suitable for treating an infected ear condition.

Do not leave an infected ear for any length of time – it could lead to a chronic condition, which can result in your dog having problems all his life, which is both painful and distressing.

NAILS

The care of toenails is often neglected, so you need to check your dog's nails on a regular basis. If a dog is given sufficient exercise on hard surfaces, his nails should wear down naturally.

However, this is not always the case, so it becomes necessary to trim back the toenails. Great care needs to be taken when trimming the nails, as if you cut off too much and damage the 'quick', it will bleed. Trim a little at a time, using canine nail clippers, which can be purchased at any good pet shop. If you are worried about trimming nails, you can ask your vet or a professional groomer to

The older dog deserves special care and attention.

do the job for you.

Dewclaws, which are located on the inside of the front legs, are often left on by the breeder. But it is better if they are removed when the puppy is four or five days old. You will need to check whether your puppy has dewclaws or not, and also check the back legs, as occasionally they appear there as well. A dewclaw can grow in a circle if it is left untrimmed; it can also grow into the leg, causing considerable pain and discomfort, and may become septic.

BATHING
A West Highland should not be bathed often; the more a Westie is bathed, the dirtier he will become. This is because shampoos tend to soften the texture of the coat and remove the natural oils. The coat then picks up the dust and dirt.

However, it may be necessary for your dog to have a bath because of a skin irritation, to eliminate parasites, or if a special shampoo has been recommended by your vet. First brush out any tangles or mats, as these will hinder the medicated shampoo reaching the skin, and then follow the instructions given by the preparation. Make sure the dog is kept warm, and if the shampoo has to remain in the coat for a period of time, wrap the dog in a warm towel until the allotted time has elapsed. As the coat dries, keep brushing so it does not dry in clumps.

If you are not using a shampoo prescribed by a vet, make sure you use a good-quality canine shampoo. If your dog is wriggly, use a baby shampoo so it will not sting his eyes. A Westie is like an elephant and will never forget – and you don't want bath times to be an ordeal for the rest of his life.

SKIN ALERT
Westies have sensitive skins and can be allergic to certain soap powders, carpets, carpet cleaning/deodorising powders, incorrect diet, pollen, fertilisers and insecticides.

CARING FOR THE OLDER DOG
Some people class a dog as a senior after seven years of age, and seek to change diet and care routines. However, the diet should not change drastically unless your dog does not get a lot of exercise. If this is the case, make sure you do not overfeed him. If he gets too fat, it will put a strain on his heart, lungs, bones and joints – and the extra pounds are very difficult to shift once gained.

You may find that an older Westie likes small meals rather than one or two a day, to help his digestion. Exercise need not be altered too much unless there is a problem. If the dog is very old, let him potter around at his own pace and don't let him walk too far – he has to get back home! If he gets wet when out walking, make sure that he is dried thoroughly when you get him

RAINBOW BRIDGE

There is a bridge connecting Heaven and Earth
It is called Rainbow Bridge because of its many colours.

Just this side of the Rainbow Bridge there is a land of meadows, hills and valleys with lush green grass.
When a beloved pet dies, the pet goes to this special place.
There is always food and water and warm spring weather.
The old and frail are young again,
Those who are maimed are made whole again.
They play all day with each other,
There is only one thing missing:
They are not with their special person who loved them on Earth.
So each day they run and play until the day comes
When one suddenly stops playing and looks up.
The nose twitches.
The ears are up.
The eyes are staring.
And this one suddenly runs from the group.

You have been seen, and when you and your special friend meet,
You take him or her into your arms and embrace, your face is kissed again and again,
And you look once more into the eyes of your trusting pet.
Then you cross the Rainbow Bridge together, never again to be separated.

Author unknown

home. He will also need a soft, comfortable and warm bed located well away from draughts.

If you have younger dogs, make sure your oldie is left in peace at times during the day. He will sleep more as the years go by and will not like to be disturbed by a youngster who wants to play when he wants to rest!

Keep your Westie clean and well groomed – an old dog should still be kept trim and smart. If his sight or hearing fail, you will find he likes to be near you all the time to give him confidence. If his sight is failing, do not move the furniture around too much, as he will be confused by changes. He might be able to see down the garden but not immediately in front of him.

Normally a West Highland will live to be about 13 years of age, sometimes less and sometimes more. But when his time does come, be guided by your vet. We all hope our beloved Westie will fade away in his basket during sleep, but this is not always the case. I always remember a grooming customer telling me that her beloved Scottie went into the garden on a summer's day and laid under his favourite shrub for a sleep and never woke up. I thought that was a lovely way for him to go over to the Rainbow Bridge.

TRAINING AND SOCIALISATION

Chapter 6

When you decided to bring a West Highland Whiter Terrier into your life, you probably had dreams of how it was going to be: long walks together, cosy evenings with a Westie sharing the sofa, and whenever you returned home, there would always be a special welcome waiting for you.

There is no doubt that you can achieve all this – and much more – with a West Highland, but like anything that is worth having, you must be prepared to put in the work. A Westie, regardless of whether it is a puppy or an adult, does not come ready trained, understanding exactly what you want and fitting perfectly into your lifestyle. A Westie has to learn his place in your family and he must discover what is

acceptable behaviour.

We have a great starting point in that the West Highland White Terrier has an outstanding temperament. The breed was developed to work on his own, catching rabbits and vermin, and in that respect he is different from a gundog, who works closely with his handler and responds instantly to commands. There are times when you will call your Westie in from the garden and he will give you a look as if to say: 'in a minute', and will carry on foraging around in the bushes. However, at the same time a Westie loves to please, and this is your trump card. Praise and reward your Westie for good behaviour, and he will thrive on the attention. He wants nothing more than to be with you; the secret is to form a close bond so that pleasing you, rather than himself, is his top priority.

THE FAMILY PACK

Dogs have been domesticated for some 14,000 years, but, luckily for us, they have inherited and retained behaviour from their distant ancestor – the wolf. A West Highland White Terrier may never have lived in the wild, but he is born with the survival skills and the mentality of a meat-eating predator who hunts in a pack. A wolf living in a pack owes its existence to mutual co-operation and an acceptance of a hierarchy, as this ensures both food and protection. A domesticated dog living in a family pack has exactly the same outlook. He wants food, companionship and leadership – and it is your job to provide for these needs.

YOUR ROLE

Theories about dog behaviour and methods of training go in and out of fashion, but, in reality,

Can you be a firm, fair and consistent leader?

nothing has changed from the day when wolves ventured in from the wild to join the family circle. The wolf (and equally the dog) accepts a subservient place in the family pack in return for food and protection. In a dog's eyes, you are his leader, and he relies on you to make all the important decisions. This does not mean that you have to act like a dictator or a bully. You are accepted as a leader, without argument, as long as you have the right credentials.

The first part of the job is easy. You are the provider, and you are therefore respected because you supply food. In a West Highland's eyes, you must be the ultimate hunter because a day never goes by when you cannot find food. The second part of the leader's job description is straightforward, but for some reason we find it hard to achieve. In order for a dog to accept his place in the family pack he must respect his leader as the decision-maker. A low-ranking pack animal does not question authority; he is perfectly happy to see someone else shoulder the responsibility. Problems will only arise if you cut a poor figure as leader and the dog feels he should mount a challenge for the top-ranking role.

HOW TO BE A GOOD LEADER

There are a number of guidelines to follow to establish yourself in the role of leader in a way that your West Highland understands and respects. If you have a puppy, you may think you don't have to take this on board for a few months, but that would be a big mistake. Start as you mean to go on, and your pup will be quick to find his place in his new family.

- **Keep it simple:** Decide on the rules you want your West Highland to obey and always make it 100 per cent clear what is acceptable, and what is unacceptable, behaviour.
- **Be consistent:** If you are not consistent about enforcing rules, how can you expect your West Highland to take you seriously? There is nothing

worse than allowing your Westie to jump up on the sofa one moment and then scolding him the next time he does it because he is muddy. As far as the Westie is concerned, he may as well try it on because he can't predict your reaction.

- **Get your timing right:** If you are rewarding your West Highland, and equally if you are reprimanding him, you must respond within one to two seconds otherwise the dog will not link his behaviour with your reaction (see page 92).

- **Read your dog's body language:** Find out how to read body language and facial expressions (see page 90) so that you understand your West Highland's feelings and his intentions.

- **Be aware of your own body language:** A dog will read your body language, and will react on what he sees. If you are calm and quiet around your West Highland, he will pick up on these vibes, and respect your unspoken authority. You can also help your dog to learn by using your body language to communicate with him. For example, if you want your Westie to come to you, open your arms out and look inviting. If you want your dog to stay, use a hand signal (palm flat, facing the dog) so you are effectively 'blocking' his advance.

- **Tone of voice:** Dogs are very receptive to tone of voice – and West Highlands more so than most. You can use your

If you get on the same wavelength as your Westie, you can build up a rapport so that he wants to work for you.

voice to praise him or to correct undesirable behaviour. If you are pleased with your Westie, praise him to the skies in a warm, happy voice. If you want to stop him raiding the bin, use a deep, stern voice when you say "No".

- **Give one command only:** If you keep repeating a command, or keep changing it, your West Highland will think you are babbling and will probably ignore you. If your Westie does not respond the first time you ask, make it simple by using a treat to lure him into position, and then you can reward him for a correct response.

- **Daily reminders:** A young, lively Westie is apt to forget his manners from time to time, and an adolescent dog may try his luck (see page 103). Rather than coming down on your Westie like a ton of bricks when he does something wrong, try to prevent bad manners by daily reminders of good manners. For example:

  i Do not let your dog barge ahead of you when you are going through a door.

  ii Do not let him leap out of the car the moment you open the door (which could be potentially lethal, as well as being disrespectful).

  iii Do not let him eat from your hand when you are at the table.

  iv Do not let him 'win' a toy at the end of a play session and then make off with it. You 'own' his toys, and you must end every play session on your terms.

UNDERSTANDING YOUR WEST HIGHLAND

Body language is an important means of communication between dogs, which they use to make friends, to assert status, and to avoid conflict. It is important to get on your dog's wavelength by understanding his body language and by reading his facial expressions.

- A positive body posture and a wagging tail indicate a happy, confident dog.

- A crouched body posture with ears back and tail down show that a dog is being submissive. A dog may do this when he is being told off or if a more assertive dog approaches him.

- A bold dog will stand tall, looking strong and alert. His ears will be forward and his tail will be held high.

- A dog who raises his hackles (lifting the fur along his topline) is trying to look as scary as possible. This may be the prelude to aggressive behaviour, but, in many cases, the dog is apprehensive and is unsure how to cope with a situation.

- A playful dog will go down on his front legs while standing on his hind legs in a bow position. This friendly invitation says: "I'm no threat, let's play."

- A dominant, aggressive dog will meet other dogs with a hard stare. If he is challenged, he may bare his teeth and growl, and the corners of his mouth will be drawn forward. His ears will be forward and he will appear tense in every muscle.

- A nervous dog will often show aggressive behaviour as a means of self-protection. If threatened, this dog will lower his head and flatten his ears. The corners of his mouth may be drawn back, and he may bark or whine.

- Some dogs are 'smilers', curling up their top lip and showing their teeth when they greet people. This should never be

In order to train your West Highland, you need to understand how his mind works.

READING THE SIGNS

These two dogs are eyeing up each other. Neither one is showing signs of aggression, but both are looking bold and assertive.

The adult (right) is giving off friendly vibes, but the youngster is taking no chances and is showing more submissive behaviour with a lowered tail and body posture.

confused with a snarl, which would be accompanied by the upright posture of a dominant dog. A smiling dog will have a low body posture and a wagging tail; he is being submissive and it is a greeting that is often used when low-ranking animals greet high-ranking animals in a pack.

GIVING REWARDS

Why should your West Highland do as you ask? If you follow the guidelines given above, your Westie should respect your authority, but what about the time when he is playing with a new doggy friend or has found a really enticing scent? The answer is that you must always be the most interesting, the most attractive, and the most irresistible person in your Westie's eyes. It would be nice to think you could achieve this by personality alone, but most of us need a little extra help. You need to find out what is the biggest reward for your dog – in a West Highland's case, it will nearly always be food – and to give him a treat when he does as you ask. For some Westies, the reward might be a play with a favourite squeaky toy but, whatever it is, it must be

TOP TREATS

Some trainers grade treats depending on what they are asking the dog to do. A dog may get a low-grade treat, such as a piece of dry food, to reward good behaviour on a random basis, such as sitting when you open a door or allowing you to examine his teeth. But high-grade treats (which, for Westies, are usually sausage or chicken), are reserved for training new exercises or for use in the park when you want a really good recall. Whatever type of treat you use, remember to subtract it from your West Highland's daily ration. Fat Westies are lethargic, prone to health problems, and will almost certainly have a shorter life expectancy. Reward your West Highland, but always keep a check on his figure!

something that your dog really wants.

When you are teaching a dog a new exercise, you should reward him frequently. When he knows the exercise or command, reward him randomly so that he keeps on responding to you in a positive manner. If your dog does something extra special, like leaving his canine chum mid-play in the park, make sure he really knows how pleased you are by giving him a handful of treats or throwing his ball a few extra times. If he gets a bonanza reward, he is more likely to come back on future occasions, because you have proved to be even more rewarding than his previous activity.

HOW DO DOGS LEARN?

It is not difficult to get inside your West Highland's head and understand how he learns, as it is not dissimilar to the way we learn. Dogs learn by conditioning: they find out that specific behaviours produce specific consequences. This is known as operant conditioning or consequence learning. Consequences have to be immediate or clearly linked to the behaviour, as a dog sees the world in terms of action and result. Dogs will quickly learn if an action has a bad consequence or a good consequence.

Dogs also learn by association. This is known as classical conditioning or association learning. It is the type of learning made famous by Pavlov's experiment with dogs. Pavlov presented dogs with food and measured their salivary response (how much they drooled). Then he rang a bell just before presenting the food. At first, the dogs did not salivate until the food was presented. But after a while they learnt that the sound of the bell meant that food was coming, and so they salivated when they heard the bell. A dog needs to learn the association in order for it to have any meaning. For example, a dog that has never seen a lead before will be

Find a training area that is free from distractions so that your Westie focuses on you.

completely indifferent to it. A dog that has learnt that a lead means he is going for a walk will get excited the second he sees the lead; he has learnt to associate a lead with a walk.

BE POSITIVE

The most effective method of training dogs is to use their ability to learn by consequence and to teach that the behaviour you want produces a good consequence. For example, if you ask your West Highland to "Sit", and reward him with a treat, he will learn that it is worth his while to sit on command because it will lead to a reward. He is far

more likely to repeat the behaviour, and the behaviour will become stronger, because it results in a positive outcome. This method of training is known as positive reinforcement, and it generally leads to a happy, co-operative dog that is willing to work, and a handler who has fun training their dog.

The opposite approach is negative reinforcement. This is far less effective and often results in a poor relationship between dog and owner. In this method of training, you ask your West Highland to "Sit", and, if he does not respond, you deliver a sharp yank on the training collar or

push his rear to the ground. The dog learns that not responding to your command has a bad consequence, and he may be less likely to ignore you in the future. However, it may well have a bad consequence for you, too. A dog that is treated in this way may associate harsh handling with the handler and become aggressive or fearful. Instead of establishing a pattern of willing co-operation, you are establishing a relationship built on coercion.

GETTING STARTED

As you train your West Highland, you will develop your own techniques as you get to know

THE CLICKER REVOLUTION

Karen Pryor pioneered the technique of clicker training when she was working with dolphins. Karen wanted to mark 'correct' behaviour at the precise moment it happened. She found that it was impossible to toss a fish to a dolphin when it was in mid-air, when she wanted to reward it. Her aim was to establish a conditioned response so the dolphin knew that it had performed correctly and a reward would follow.

The solution was the clicker: a small matchbox-shaped training aid, with a metal tongue that makes a click when it is pressed. To begin with, the dolphin had to learn that a click meant that food was coming. The dolphin then learnt that it must 'earn' a click in order to get a reward. Clicker training has been used with many different animals, most particularly with dogs, and it has proved hugely successful. It is a great aid for pet owners and is also widely used by professional trainers teaching highly specialised skills.

what motivates him. You may decide to get involved with clicker training or you may prefer to go for a simple command-and-reward formula. It does not matter what form of training you use, as long as it is based on positive, reward-based methods.

There are a few important guidelines to bear in mind when you are training your West Highland White:

- Start training from an early age. The West Highland may be small in stature, but he is big in personality, and he needs to be trained just as much as a larger dog.
- Find a training area that is free from distractions, particularly when you are just starting out.

- Keep training sessions short, especially with young puppies that have very short attention spans.
- Do not train if you are in a bad mood or if you are on a tight schedule – the training session will be doomed to failure.
- If you are using a toy as a reward, make sure it is only available when you are training. In this way it has an added value for your West Highland.
- If you are using food treats, make sure they are bite-size and easy to swallow; you don't want to hang about while your Westie chews on his treat.

- All food treats must be deducted from your Westie's daily food ration.
- When you are training, move around your allocated area so that your West Highland does not think that an exercise can only be performed in one place.
- If your West Highland is finding an exercise difficult, try not to get frustrated. Go back a step and praise him for his effort. You will probably find he is more successful when you try again at the next training session.
- Always end training sessions on a happy, positive note. Ask your West Highland to do something you know he can

do – it could be a trick he enjoys performing – and then reward him with a few treats or an extra-long play session.
- Most important of all – make training sessions fun!

In the exercises that follow, clicker training is introduced and followed, but all the exercises will work without the use of a clicker.

INTRODUCING A CLICKER

This is dead easy, and a West Highland who loves his food will learn about the clicker in record time. It can be combined with attention training, which is a very useful tool and can be used on many different occasions.

- Prepare some treats and go to an area that is free from distractions. When your West Highland stops sniffing around and looks at you, click and reward by throwing him a treat. This means he will not crowd you, but will go looking for the treat. Repeat a couple of times. If your Westie is very easily distracted, you may need to start this exercise with the dog on a lead.
- After a few clicks, your West Highland understands that if he hears a click, he will get a treat. He must now learn that he must 'earn' a click. This time, when your West Highland looks at you, wait a little longer before clicking, and then reward him. If your Westie is on a lead but responding well, try him off the lead.

- When your West Highland is working for a click and giving you his attention, you can introduce a cue or command word, such as "Watch". Repeat a few times, using the cue. You now have a Westie that understands the clicker and will give you his attention when you ask him to "Watch".

TRAINING EXERCISES

THE SIT

This is the easiest exercise to teach, so it is rewarding for both you and your West Highland.

- Choose a tasty treat and hold it just above your puppy's nose. As he looks up at the treat, he will naturally go into the Sit.

Initially, train the Sit by luring with a treat, and then progress to using a verbal command.

Lower a treat to the ground and your Westie will follow it, going into the Down position.

Work on getting an enthusiastic response to the Recall.

As soon as he is in position, reward him.

- Repeat the exercise, and when your pup understands what you want, introduce the "Sit" command.
- You can practise at mealtimes by holding out the bowl and waiting for your dog to sit. Most West Highland White Terriers learn this one very quickly!

THE DOWN

Work hard at this exercise because a reliable Down is useful in many different situations, and an instant Down can be a lifesaver.

- You can start with your dog in a Sit, or it is just as effective to teach it when the dog is standing. Hold a treat just below your puppy's nose, and slowly lower it towards the ground. The treat acts as a lure, and your puppy will follow it, first going down on his forequarters, and then bringing his hindquarters down as he tries to get the treat.
- Make sure you close your fist around the treat, and only reward your puppy with the treat when he is in the correct position. If your puppy is reluctant to go Down, you can apply gentle pressure on his

shoulders to encourage him to go into the correct position.

- When your puppy is following the treat and going in to position, introduce a verbal command.
- Build up this exercise over a period of time, each time waiting a little longer before giving the reward, so the puppy learns to stay in the Down position.

THE RECALL

It is never too soon to start training the Recall. The West Highland has a strong sense of smell, and he is always eager to hunt and chase. It is therefore

SECRET WEAPON

You can build up a strong Recall by using another form of association learning. Buy a whistle, and when you are giving your West Highland his food, peep on the whistle. You can choose the type of signal you want to give: two short peeps, or one long whistle, for example. Within a matter of days, your dog will learn that the sound of the whistle means that food is coming.

Now transfer the lesson outside. Arm yourself with some tasty treats and the whistle. Allow your Westie to run free in the garden, and, after a couple of minutes, use the whistle. The dog has already learnt to associate the whistle with food, so he will come towards you. Immediately

reward him with a treat and lots of praise. Repeat the lesson a few times in the garden so you are confident that your dog is responding before trying it in the park. Make sure you always have some treats in your pocket when you go for a walk, and your dog will quickly learn how rewarding it is to come to you.

important to train your dog that it is always rewarding to come to you rather than to follow his own agenda.

- If you have a puppy, it is best to start Recall training almost from the moment the puppy arrives home, as he will instinctively want to follow you. Make sure you are always happy and excited when your West Highland comes to you, even if he has been slower than you would like.
- Practise in the garden, and, when your puppy is busy exploring, get his attention by calling his name. As he runs towards you, introduce the verbal command "Come". Make sure you sound happy

and exciting, so your puppy wants to come to you. When he responds, give him lots of praise, and reward him with a tasty treat.

- If your puppy is slow to respond, try running away a few paces, or jumping up and down. It doesn't matter how silly you look, the key issue is to get your puppy's attention – and then make yourself irresistible!
- In a dog's mind, coming when called should be regarded as the best fun because he knows he is always going to be rewarded. Never make the mistake of telling your dog off, no matter how slow he is to respond, as you will undo all your previous hard work.

- When you are free-running your dog, make sure you have his favourite toy, or a pocket full of treats so you can reward him at intervals throughout the walk when you call him to you. Do not allow your dog to free run and only call him back at the end of the walk to clip on his lead. An intelligent West Highland will soon realise that the Recall means the end of his walk, and then end of fun – so who can blame him for not wanting to come back?

The biggest mistake is to let your West Highland off-lead before he has a reliable response to the Recall. If your dog gets into the habit of ignoring you or running off, you will find it very difficult to

is to prevent your Westie from disobeying you so that he never has the chance to get into bad habits. For example, when you call your Westie and he ignores you, you can immediately pick up the end of the training line and call him again. By picking up the line, you will have attracted his attention, and if you call in an excited, happy voice, your Westie will come to you. The moment he comes to you, give him a tasty treat so he is instantly rewarded for making the 'right' decision.

WALKING ON A LOOSE LEAD
This simple exercise baffles many West Highland owners. In most cases, owners are too impatient, wanting to get on with the expedition rather that training the dog how to walk on a lead. Take time with this one: a Westie that pulls or drags on the lead is no pleasure to own.

- Make lead training fun. Start by going in the garden, and simply having a game with the lead so that your Westie builds up a good association with it.
- In the early stages of lead training, attach the lead to the collar and allow your puppy to pick his route and follow him. He will get used to the feeling of being 'attached' to you, and has no reason to put up any resistance. Let him walk for a few paces, and then have a game.
- Next, find a toy or a tasty treat and show it to your puppy. Let him follow the treat or toy for a few paces, and then reward

A perfect example of a Westie walking on a loose lead, giving attention to his owner when requested.

retrain him. The best plan is practise in the garden, always rewarding your Westie when he comes to you. Then, when he is about six months old, you can try free-running him, as, by this time, he will have built up a strong response to the Recall, and it will not occur to him to ignore you.

TRAINING LINE
This is the equivalent of a very long lead, which you can buy at a pet store, or you can make your own with a length of rope. The training line is attached to your West Highland's collar and should be around 15 feet (4.5 metres) in length.

The purpose of the training line

him or have a game.

- Build up the amount of time your pup will walk with you, and, when he is walking nicely by your side, introduce the verbal command "Heel" or "Close". Give lots of praise when your pup is in the correct position.

- When your pup is walking alongside you, keep focusing his attention on you by using his name, and then reward him when he looks at you. If it is going well, introduce some changes of direction.

- Do not attempt to take your puppy out on the lead until you have mastered the basics at home. You need to be confident that your puppy accepts the lead and will focus his attention on you, when requested, before you face the challenge of a busy environment.

- As your West Highland becomes more confident, he may try to pull on the lead, particularly if you are heading somewhere he wants to go, such as the park. If this happens, stop, call your dog to you, and do not set off again until he is in the correct position. It may take time, but your Westie will eventually realise that it is more productive to walk by your side than to pull ahead.

The West Highland has a stubborn streak, and this can come to the fore if lead training becomes confrontational. The last thing you want is to have a

The Stay exercise can be built up in easy stages.

Westie that drags on the lead, or one that goes in for sit-down strikes. The key is to make your West Highland believe that lead training is all part of a game. Keep the mood light-hearted and positive, and you will soon have a Westie that trots along happily beside you.

STAYS

This may not be the most exciting exercise, but it is one of the most useful. There are many occasions when you want your West Highland to stay in position, even if it is only for a few seconds. The classic example is when you want your Westie to stay in the back of the car until you have clipped on his lead. Some trainers use the verbal

command "Stay" when the dog is to stay in position for an extended period of time, and "Wait" if the dog is to stay in position for a few seconds until you give the next command. Others trainers use a universal "Stay" to cover all situations. It all comes down to personal preference, and as long as you are consistent, your dog will understand the command he is given.

- Put your puppy in a Sit or a Down, and use a hand signal (flat palm, facing the dog) to show he is to stay in position. Step a pace away from the dog. Wait a second, step back and reward him. If you have a lively pup, you may find it

A young puppy will soak up new experiences like a sponge.

easier to train this exercise on the lead.

- Repeat the exercise, gradually increasing the distance you can leave your dog. When you return to your dog's side, praise him quietly and release him with a command, such as "OK".
- Remember to keep your body language very still when you are training this exercise, and avoid eye contact with your dog. Work on this exercise over a period of time, and you will build up a really reliable Stay.

SOCIALISATION

While your West Highland White Terrier is mastering basic obedience exercises, there is other, equally important, work to do with him. A Westie is not only becoming a part of your home and family, he is becoming a member of the community. He needs to be able to live in the outside world, coping calmly with every new situation that comes his way. It is your job to introduce him to as many different experiences as possible and to encourage him to behave in an appropriate manner.

In order to socialise your Westie effectively, it is helpful to understand how his brain is developing, and then you will get a perspective on how he sees the world.

CANINE SOCIALISATION
(Birth to 7 weeks)
This is the time when a dog learns how to be a dog. By interacting with his mother and his littermates, a young pup learns about leadership and submission. He learns to read body posture so that he understands the intentions of his mother and his siblings. A puppy that is taken away from his litter too early may always have behavioural problems with other dogs, either being fearful or aggressive.

SOCIALISATION PERIOD
(7 to 12 weeks)
This is the time to get cracking and introduce your West Highland puppy to as many different experiences as possible. This includes meeting different people, other dogs and animals, seeing new sights, and hearing a range of sounds, from the vacuum cleaner to the roar of traffic. At this stage, a puppy

learns very quickly and what he learns will stay with him for the rest of his life. This is the best time for a puppy to move to a new home, as he is adaptable and ready to form deep bonds.

FEAR-IMPRINT PERIOD
(8 to 11 weeks)

This occurs during the socialisation period, and it can be the cause of problems if it is not handled carefully. If a pup is exposed to a frightening or painful experience, it will lead to lasting impressions. Obviously, you will attempt to avoid frightening situations, such as your pup being bullied by a mean-spirited older dog, or a firework going off, but you cannot always protect your puppy from the unexpected. If your pup has a nasty experience, the best plan is to make light of it and distract him by offering him a treat or a game. The pup will take the lead from you and will be reassured that there is nothing to worry about. If you mollycoddle him and sympathise with him, he is far more likely to retain the memory of his fear.

SENIORITY PERIOD
(12 to 16 weeks)

During this period, your West Highland puppy starts to cut the apron strings and becomes more independent. He will test out his status to find out who is the pack leader: him or you. Bad habits, such as play biting, which may have been seen as endearing a few weeks earlier, should be firmly discouraged. Remember to

A well-socialised West Highland will be calm and confident in different environments.

use positive, reward-based training, but make sure your puppy knows that you are the leader and must be respected.

SECOND FEAR-IMPRINT PERIOD
(6 to 14 months)

This period is not as critical as the first fear-imprint period, but it should still be handled carefully. During this time your Westie may appear apprehensive, or he may show fear of something familiar. You may feel as if you have taken a backwards step, but if you adopt a calm, positive manner,

your Westie will see that there is nothing to be frightened of. Do not make your dog confront the thing that frightens him. Simply distract his attention and give him something else to think about, such as obeying a simple command, such as "Sit" or "Down". This will give you the opportunity to praise and reward your dog, and will help to boost his confidence.

YOUNG ADULTHOOD AND MATURITY (1 to 4 years)

The timing of this phase depends on the size of the dog: the bigger the dog, the later it is. This period coincides with a dog's increasing maturity, mental as well as physical. Some dogs, particularly those with a dominant nature, will test your leadership again and may become aggressive towards other dogs. Firmness and continued training are essential at this time so that your West Highland accepts his status in the family pack.

IDEAS FOR SOCIALISATION
When you are socialising your West Highland, you want him to experience as many different situations as possible. Try out some of the following ideas, which will ensure your Westie has an all-round education.

If you are taking on a rescued dog and have little knowledge of his background, it is important to work through a programme of socialisation. A young puppy soaks up new experiences like a sponge, but an older dog can still learn. If a rescued dog shows fear or apprehension, treat him in exactly the same way as you would treat a youngster who is going through the second fear-imprint period (see page 101).

- Accustom your puppy to household noises, such as the vacuum cleaner, the television and the washing machine.
- Ask visitors to come to the door, wearing different types of clothing – for example, wearing a hat or a long raincoat, or carrying a stick or an umbrella.

- If you do not have children at home, make sure your Westie has a chance to meet and play with them. Go to a local park and watch children in the play area. You will not be able to take your Westie inside the play area, but he will see children playing and will get used to their shouts of excitement.
- Attend puppy classes. These are designed for puppies between the ages of 12 to 20 weeks, and give pups a chance to play and interact together in a controlled, supervised environment. Your vet will have details of a local class.
- Take a walk around some quiet streets, such as a residential area, so your West Highland can get used to the sound of

TRAINING CLUBS

There are lots of training clubs to choose from. Your vet will probably have details of clubs in your area, or you can ask friends who have dogs if they attend a club. Alternatively, use the internet to find out more information. But how do you know if the club is any good?

Before you take your dog, ask if you can go to a class as an observer and find out the following:
- What experience does the instructor(s) have?
- Do they have experience with West Highland White Terriers?
- Is the class well organised, and are the dogs

reasonably quiet? (A noisy class indicates an unruly atmosphere, which will not be conducive to learning.)
- Are there are a number of classes to suit dogs of different ages and abilities?
- Are positive, reward-based training methods used?
- Does the club train for the Good Citizen Scheme? (see page 110)

If you are not happy with the training club, find another one. An inexperienced instructor who cannot handle a number of dogs in a confined environment can do more harm than good.

traffic. As he becomes more confident, progress to busier areas.

- Go to a railway station. You don't have to get on a train if you don't need to, but your West Highland will have the chance to experience trains, people wheeling luggage, loudspeaker announcements, and going up and down stairs and over railway bridges.
- If you live in the town, plan a trip to the country. You can enjoy a day out and provide an opportunity for your West Highland to see livestock, such as sheep, cattle and horses.
- One of the best places for socialising a dog is at a country fair. There will be crowds of people, livestock in pens, tractors, bouncy castles, fairground rides and food stalls.
- When your dog is over 20 weeks of age, find a training class for adult dogs. You may find that your local training class has both puppy and adult classes.

THE ADOLESCENT WEST HIGHLAND

It happens to every dog – and every owner. One minute you have an obedient well-behaved youngster, and the next you have an adolescent who appears to have forgotten everything he learnt. This applies equally to males and females, although the type of adolescent behaviour, and its onset, varies between individuals.

In most cases a West Highland male will hit adolescence at around eight to 10 months, and

When a West Highland hits adolescence you can expect some behavioural changes.

you can expect behavioural changes for at least a couple of months. In most cases, a male Westie will not change dramatically in personality at this time, particularly in relation to people. However, he may pay more attention to bitches, and he may attempt to be more assertive with other male dogs. It is very much a time when the adolescent male is feeling his feet and finding his place in the adult dog world.

Female West Highlands show adolescent behaviour between seven and 10 months – this usually coincides with the onset of the first season. At this time, a female Westie may become

quieter than usual; she may seem a little withdrawn and off-colour. She may become more sensitive, and she will often be shy with other dogs – particularly if they are over assertive.

This is a trying time in a dog's life, and it can be slightly stressful to have a dog who is acting out of character. However, it is important to remember that it is only a passing phase on the journey to becoming a fully fledged adult. Try not to react to mood swings or 'laddish' behaviour. Adopt a sensible no-nonsense approach – and your West Highland will soon get over his teenage phase.

WHEN THINGS GO WRONG

Positive, reward-based training has proved to be the most effective method of teaching dogs, but what happens when your West Highland does something wrong and you need to show him that his behaviour is unacceptable? The old-fashioned school of dog training used to rely on the powers of punishment and negative reinforcement. A dog who raided the bin, for example, was smacked. Now we have learnt that it is not only unpleasant and cruel to hit a dog, it is also ineffective. If you hit a dog for stealing, he is more than likely to see you as the bad consequence of stealing, so he may raid the bin again, but probably not when you are around. If he raided the bin some time before you discovered it, he will be even more confused by your punishment, as he will not relate your response to his 'crime'.

A more commonplace example is when a dog fails to respond to a recall in the park. When the dog eventually comes back, the owner puts the dog on the lead and goes straight home to punish the dog for his poor response. Unfortunately, the dog will have a different interpretation. He does not think: "I won't ignore a recall command because the bad consequence is the end of my play in the park." He thinks: "Coming to my owner resulted in the end of playtime – therefore coming to my owner has a bad consequence, so I won't do that again."

There are a number of strategies to tackle undesirable behaviour – and they have nothing to do with harsh handling.

Ignoring bad behaviour

A lot of undesirable behaviour in young West Highland White Terriers should be blamed on their owners. If an intelligent Westie gets away with jumping up at you, or barking at you in order to get your attention, he will continue doing it. In no time, this will become habit forming – and you will find it very hard to retrain him.

The key is to get in early so that your West Highland learns that his attention-seeking strategies are not working. For example, if your West Highland likes the sound of his own voice, do not react by shouting at him, telling him to be quiet. As far as a West Highland is concerned, he has got what he wanted – your attention. You are joining in a 'conversation' with him, regardless of how loud you are shouting. So, if your Westie starts barking, ignore him. Avoid eye contact and turn your back on him. The moment he is quiet, you can call him to you and give lots of praise and maybe a treat. You can also focus his attention by having a game with a toy or doing a simple training exercise. If a West Highland is engaged with you, he will have no need to bark, as he has your attention.

You may have to work on this over a period of time, but a West Highland is a smart, quick-witted dog who picks things up easily. It will not take him long to realise that barking gets no response, whereas being quiet earns him a bonanza reward. Being ignored is a worst-case scenario for a West Highland, so remember to use it as an effective training tool.

Stopping bad behaviour

There are occasions when you want to call an instant halt to whatever it is your West Highland is doing. He may have just jumped on the sofa, or you may have caught him red-handed in the

There are times when you catch your Westie red-handed, and you need to call an instant halt to his behaviour.

rubbish bin. He has already committed the 'crime', so your aim is to stop him and to redirect his attention. You can do this by using a deep, firm tone of voice to say "No", which will startle him, and then call him to you in a bright, happy voice. If necessary, you can attract him with a toy or a treat. The moment your West Highland stops the undesirable behaviour and comes towards you, you can reward his good behaviour. You can back this up by running through a couple of simple exercises, such as a Sit or a Down, and rewarding with treats. In this way, your Westie focuses his attention on you and sees you as the greatest source of reward and pleasure.

In a more extreme situation, when you want to interrupt undesirable behaviour, and you know that a simple "No" will not do the trick, you can try something a little more dramatic. If you get a can and fill it with pebbles, it will make a really loud noise when you shake it or throw it. The same effect can be achieved with purpose-made training discs. The dog will be startled and will stop what he is doing. Even better, the dog will not associate the unpleasant noise with you. This gives you the perfect opportunity to be the nice guy, calling the dog to you and giving him lots of praise.

PROBLEM BEHAVIOUR

If you have trained your West Highland from puppyhood, survived his adolescence and established yourself as a fair and consistent leader, you will end up with a brilliant companion dog. The West Highland White Terrier is a well-balanced, friendly dog who is eager to please and rarely has hang-ups. Most Westies are lively and intelligent, and thrive on spending time with their owners.

However, problems may arise unexpectedly, or you may have taken on a rescued West Highland that has established behavioural problems. If you are worried about your Westie and feel out of your depth, do not delay in seeking professional help. This is readily available, usually through a referral from your vet, or you can find out additional information on the internet (see Appendices for web addresses). An animal behaviourist will have experience in tackling problem behaviour and will be able to help both you and your dog.

MOUTHING

Puppies explore the world with their mouths and with their noses. They pick up different scents, and if they come across something new, they will investigate by using their mouth and teeth. Littermates will play together, mouthing and biting each other, and they will often play with their mother in the same way. Crucially, a puppy learns to stop biting if his mother or a littermate let out a shriek of pain, or growl a warning.

When a puppy arrives in his new home, he will still want to explore by mouthing. It is your job to show him, right from the start, that mouthing, nibbling or nipping people is unacceptable. It is vitally important to do this from day one so your puppy does not learn to assert his will by biting. Problems have arisen with

West Highlands who have been poorly socialised, with little handling. Their response to something they don't like, such as grooming, is to turn and nip. This is not typical Westie behaviour; it is the consequence of a poor upbringing.

The best way of inhibiting mouthing or nipping is to copy what the puppy has already learnt in the nest while he was growing up with his siblings:

- If your Westie tries to mouth or nip, give a sharp cry so he realises he has stepped out of line.
- Then offer him a treat in the palm of your hand and ask him to take it "Gently".
- Keep repeating this exercise so your West Highland learns that it is more rewarding to stop mouthing. He will see that a hand is offering him a treat rather than seeing it as fingers to nibble.
- If you have children, supervise all interactions to make sure your Westie is not getting over-excited and resorting to mouthing.

If you have taken on a rescued dog that has mouthing or nipping problems, you may need to seek professional advice.

SEPARATION ANXIETY

The West Highland White Terrier will not thrive if he is left for long periods on his own, but he should be able to tolerate some time alone without becoming stressed. A new puppy should be

In the first instance, it is the mother who will reprimand a puppy for stepping out of line.

If a West Highland is not accustomed to spending some time alone, he may become anxious.

A baby-gate can act as a halfway house when you are working on separation anxiety, allowing your dog to cope on his own while you are still in sight.

left for short periods on his own, ideally in a crate where he cannot get up to any mischief. It is a good idea to leave him with a boredom-busting toy (such as a Kong) so he will be happily occupied in your absence. When you return, do not rush to the crate and make a huge fuss. Wait a few minutes, and then calmly go to the crate and release your dog, telling him how good he has been. If this scenario is repeated a number of times, your Westie will soon learn that being left on his own is no big deal.

Problems with separation anxiety are most likely to arise if you take on a rescued dog who has major insecurities. You may also find that your West Highland hates being left if you have failed to accustom him to short periods of isolation when he was growing up. Separation anxiety is

expressed in a number of ways, and all are equally distressing for both dog and owner. An anxious dog who is left alone may bark and whine continuously, urinate and defecate, and may be extremely destructive.

There are a number of steps you can take when attempting to solve this problem.

• Put up a baby-gate between adjoining rooms, and leave your dog in one room while you are in the other room. Your dog will be able to see you and hear you, but he is learning to cope without being right next to you. Build up the amount of time you can leave your dog in easy stages.
• Buy some boredom-busting toys and fill them with some tasty treats. Whenever you leave your dog, give him a

food-filled toy so that he is busy while you are away.
• If you have not used a crate before, it is not too late to start. Make sure the crate is big and comfortable, and train your West Highland to get used to going in his crate while you are in the same room. Gradually build up the amount of time he spends in the crate, and then start leaving the room for short periods. When you return, do not make a fuss of your dog. Leave him for five or 10 minutes before releasing him so that he gets used to your comings and goings.
• Pretend to go out, putting on your coat and jangling keys, but do not leave the house. An anxious dog often becomes hyped up by the ritual of leave taking, so this will help to desensitise him.

- When you go out, leave a radio or a TV on. Some dogs are comforted by hearing voices and background noise when they are left alone.
- Try to make your absences as short as possible when you are first training your dog to accept being on his own. When you return, do not fuss your dog, rushing to his crate to release him. Leave him for a few minutes, and when you go to him remain calm and relaxed so that he does not become hyped up with a huge greeting.

If you take these steps, your dog should become less anxious, and, over a period of time, you should be able to solve the problem. However, if you are failing to make progress, do not delay in calling in expert help.

RESOURCE GUARDING
The West Highland Terrier is rarely domineering in his behaviour, but he is a clever dog who is capable of manipulating situations to his advantage. A West Highland may find something he wants, and then becoming possessive in order to guard what he sees as a valuable resource. This may take a number of different forms:

- A West Highland may become possessive over his food bowl and growl if you approach him when he is eating.
- He may adopt a favourite toy and refuse to give it up when requested.
- He may decide that the sofa is the best place to lie, and growl a warning if you ask him to move.

If you see signs of your West Highland becoming manipulative, you must work at lowering his status so that he realises that you are the leader and he does not have the right to guard resources.

Although you need to be firm, you also need to use positive training methods so that your Westie is rewarded for the behaviour you want. In this way, his 'correct' behaviour will be strengthened and repeated.

There are a number of steps you can take to teach your West Highland that you are in control. They include:

- Go back to basics and hold daily training sessions. Make sure you have some really tasty treats, or find a toy your West Highland really values and only bring it out at training sessions. Run through all the training exercises, and make a big fuss of your Westie, rewarding him when he does well. This will reinforce the message that you are the leader and that it is rewarding to do as you ask.
- Teach your West Highland something new; this can be as simple as learning a trick, such as shaking paws. Having something new to think about will stimulate your West Highland, and he will benefit from interacting with you.
- Be 100 per cent consistent with all house rules – your West Highland must never sit on the sofa (reward him for lying on his bed or on the floor) and you must never allow him to jump up at you (reward him for sitting when he greets you). This will make him more likely to repeat the desired behaviour.
- If your West Highland has been

Sometimes a Westie will become possessive over a toy and be reluctant to give it up.

guarding his food bowl, put the bowl down empty, and drop in a little food at a time. Periodically stop dropping in the food, and tell your Westie to "Sit" and "Wait". Give it a few seconds, and then reward him by dropping in more food. He will quickly learn that having you around at mealtimes is a good thing.

- Make sure the family eats before you feed your West Highland. Some trainers advocate eating in front of the dog (maybe just a few bites from a biscuit) before starting a training session, so the dog appreciates your elevated status.
- Do not let your Westie barge through doors ahead of you or leap from the back of the car before you release him. You may need to put your dog on the lead and teach him to "Wait" at doorways, and then reward him for letting you go through first.

If your West Highland is progressing well with his retraining programme, think about getting involved with a dog sport, such as agility or flyball. This will give your Westie a positive outlet for his energies. However, if your West Highland is still resource guarding, or you have any other concerns, do not delay in seeking the help of an animal behaviourist.

AGGRESSION
Aggression is a complex issue, as there are different causes and the behaviour may be triggered by

It is rare for a West Highland White Terrier to be aggressive with other dogs.

numerous factors. It may be directed towards people, but far more commonly it is directed towards other dogs. Aggression in dogs may be the result of:
- Assertive behaviour.
- Defensive behaviour: This may be induced by fear, pain or punishment.
- Territory: A dog may become aggressive if strange dogs or people enter his territory (which is generally seen as the house and garden).
- Intra-sexual issues: This is aggression between sexes – male-to-male or female-to-female.
- Parental instinct: A mother dog may become aggressive if she is protecting her puppies.

A dog who has been well socialised (see page 100) and has been given sufficient exposure to other dogs at significant stages of his development will rarely be aggressive. A well-bred West Highland that has been reared correctly should not have a hint of aggression in his temperament. Obviously, if you have taken on an older, rescued dog, you will have little or no knowledge of his background, and if he shows signs of aggression, the cause will need to be determined. In most cases, you would be well advised to call in professional help if you see aggressive behaviour in your dog; if the aggression is directed towards people, you should seek immediate advice. This behaviour can escalate very quickly and could lead to disastrous consequences.

NEW CHALLENGES

If you enjoy training your West Highland White Terrier, you may want to try one of the many dog sports that are now on offer.

GOOD CITIZEN SCHEME

This is a scheme run by the Kennel Club in the UK and the American Kennel Club in the USA. The schemes promote responsible ownership and help you to train a well-behaved dog who will fit in with the community. The schemes are excellent for all pet owners, and they are also a good starting point if you plan to compete with your West Highland when he is older. The KC and the AKC schemes vary in format. In the UK there are three levels: bronze, silver and gold, with each test becoming progressively more demanding. In the AKC scheme there is a single test.

Some of the exercises include:
- Walking on a loose lead among people and other dogs.
- Recall amid distractions.
- A controlled greeting where dogs stay under control while owners meet.
- The dog allows all-over grooming and handling by his owner, and also accepts being handled by the examiner.
- Stays, with the owner in sight, and then out of sight.

The intelligent Westie will thrive on new training challenges.

- Food manners, allowing the owner to eat without begging, and taking a treat on command.
- Sendaway – sending the dog to his bed.

The tests are designed to show the control you have over your dog, and his ability to respond correctly and remain calm in all situations. The Good Citizen Scheme is taught at most training clubs. For more information, log on to the Kennel Club or AKC website (see Appendices).

SHOWING

In your eyes, your West Highland is the most beautiful dog in the world – but would a judge agree?

Showing is a highly competitive sport, and the West Highland must be correctly presented, which can be very time-consuming. However, many owners get bitten by the showing bug, and their calendar is governed by the dates of the top showing fixtures.

To be successful in the show ring, a West Highland White Terrier must conform as closely as possible to the Breed Standard, which is a written blueprint describing the 'perfect' West Highland (see Chapter Seven). To get started you need to buy a puppy that has show potential and then train him to perform in the ring. A Westie will be expected to stand in show pose, gait for the judge in order to show off his natural movement, and to be examined by the judge. This involves a detailed hands-on examination, so your West Highland must be bombproof when handled by strangers.

Many training clubs hold ringcraft classes, which are run by experienced showgoers. At these classes, you will learn how to handle your West Highland in the ring, and you will also find out about rules, procedures and show ring etiquette.

Showing is highly competitive at the top level.

Training for competitive obedience with a West Highland is not easy, but it can be done.

The best plan is to start off at some small, informal shows where you can practise and learn the tricks of the trade before graduating to bigger shows. It's a long haul starting in the very first puppy class, but the dream is to make your West Highland up into a Champion.

COMPETITIVE OBEDIENCE

Border Collies and German Shepherds dominate this sport, with gundog breeds making up the numbers. However, the West Highland is an intelligent dog, and if you work on motivation and focusing his attention, there is no reason why you should not have a go at this sport. It is possible to obedience train a Westie to a fairly high level depending on the capability of

the owner – but his terrier temperament and independent character should always be taken into consideration.

The classes start off being relatively easy and become progressively more challenging, with additional exercises and the handler giving minimal instructions to the dog.

Exercises include:

- **Heelwork:** Dog and handler must complete a set pattern on and off the lead, which includes left turns, right turns, about turns, and changes of pace.
- **Recall:** This may be when the handler is stationary or on the move.
- **Retrieve:** This may be a dumbbell or any article

chosen by the judge.
- **Sendaway:** The dog is sent to a designated spot and must go into an instant Down until he is recalled by the handler.
- **Stays:** The dog must stay in the Sit and in the Down for a set amount of time. In advanced classes, the handler is out of sight,
- **Scent:** The dog must retrieve a single cloth from a pre-arranged pattern of cloths that has his owner's scent, or, in advanced classes, the judge's scent. There may also be decoy cloths.
- **Distance control.** The dog must execute a series of moves (Sit, Stand, Down) without moving from his position and with the handler at a distance.

THE AGILE WESTIE

Powering through the tunnel.

Clearing the jumps.

Even though competitive obedience requires accuracy and precision, make it fun for your Westie, with lots of praise and rewards so that you motivate him to do his best. Many training clubs run advanced classes for those who want to compete in obedience, or you can hire the services of a professional trainer for one-on-one sessions.

AGILITY
This fun sport has grown enormously in popularity over the past few years. If you fancy having a go, make sure you have good control over your West Highland and keep him slim. Agility is a very physical sport, which demands fitness from both dog and handler. A fat Westie is never going to make it as an agility competitor.

In agility competitions, each dog must complete a set course over a series of obstacles, which include:

• Jumps (upright hurdles and long jump)
• Weaves
• A-frame
• Dog walk
• Seesaw
• Tunnels (collapsible and rigid)
• Tyre

Dogs may compete in Jumping classes with jumps, tunnels and weaves, or in Agility classes, which have the full set of equipment. Faults are awarded for poles down on the jumps, missed contact points on the A-frame, dog walk and seesaw, and refusals. If a dog takes the wrong course, he is eliminated. The winner is the dog that completes the course in the fastest time with no faults. As you progress up the levels, courses become progressively harder with more twists, turns and changes of direction.

If you want to get involved in agility, you will need to find a club that specialises in the sport (see Appendices). You will not be allowed to start training until your West Highland is 12 months old, and you cannot compete until he is 18 months old. This rule is for the protection of the dog, who may suffer injury if he puts strain on bones and joints while he is still growing.

FLYBALL
West Highland White Terriers are not natural retrievers, but, surprisingly, some really take to

flyball. Flyball is a team sport; the dogs love it, and it is undoubtedly the noisiest of all the canine sports!

Four dogs are selected to run in a relay race against an opposing team. The dogs are sent out by their handlers to jump four hurdles, catch the ball from the flyball box, and then return over the hurdles. At the top level, this sport is fast and furious, and although it is dominated by Border Collies, the West Highland can still make a contribution. This is particularly true in multibreed competitions where the team is made up of four dogs of different breeds, and only one can be a Border Collie or a Working Sheepdog. Points are awarded to dogs and teams. Annual awards are given to top dogs and top teams, and milestone awards are given out to dogs as they attain points throughout their flyballing careers.

EARTH DOG TESTS

In America, terriers can take part in earth dog tests, and many Westies have excelled in this sport. The aim is to test a terrier's natural hunting instinct by sending him into a tunnel to follow a scent and find a quarry. The test become increasingly complex with false scent trails, and bends and turns within the

If you spend quality time with your Westie, you will develop a very special bond.

tunnel, as a terrier graduates through the ranks from junior to senior, and finally to master earth dog. Earth dog tests are one of the most relaxing and enjoyable activities you can do with your Westie.

TRACKING

In the US, dogs can also take part in tracking, which is run as a discipline in its own right. In fact, tracking is what our dogs often do when they are out for a walk. They detect the scents of various animals and people as they walk, and often they try to follow the ones that interest them. In tracking events, you train your dog to follow a scent you choose for them. Tracking is definitely a sport at which Westies can excel, because they were bred to hunt

using their noses to help them find their quarry.

DANCING WITH DOGS

This sport is relatively new, but it is becoming increasingly popular. It is very entertaining to watch, but it is certainly not as simple as it looks. To perform a choreographed routine to music with your West Highland demands a huge amount of training.

Dancing with dogs is divided into two categories: heelwork to music and canine freestyle. In heelwork to music, the dog must work closely with his handler and show a variety of close 'heelwork' positions. In canine freestyle, the routine can be more flamboyant, with the dog working at a distance from the handler and performing spectacular tricks. Routines are judged on style and presentation, content and accuracy.

SUMMING UP

The West Highland White Terrier has it all – he is quick-witted, full of character, and is a fun and loving companion. Make sure you keep your half of the bargain: spend time socialising and training your Westie so that you can be proud to take him anywhere and he will always be a credit to you.

WONDER WESTIES

There are those that say that West Highland White Terriers cannot be trained, but Holly Jane Barrington and her Westies are living proof that this is a breed that can be trained to a high level in a variety of disciplines.

Holly lives in Thornbury, Gloucestershire. Her mother used to own Poodles, but when Holly was 10, they purchased their first Westie – His Masters Choice at McHolglyn, known as Bertie.

"When we bought our first puppy, we enrolled in what we thought was a puppy obedience class," said Holly. "But, by accident, we ended up going to a ringcraft class instead. We loved the classes so much that we took it a step further and joined

Bertie (His Masters Choice at McHolglyn) was Holly's first Westie.

a ringcraft class in Gloucestershire that specialised in junior handling."

BITTEN BY THE BUG

It did not take long for the showing bug to bite, and soon Holly was entering companion dog show handling classes, then open, and then Championship handling classes. Holly proved to be a natural handler and she and Bertie have enjoyed considerable success, qualifying for Crufts each year and getting highly placed in stakes classes at Crufts.

The next Westie to join the Barrington family was Cabon Sea Maiden at McHolyglyn, known as Kizzy. She proved to be a real star in the show ring. She regularly qualifies for Crufts, and gained her stud book number after winning first in a large limit class.

"Kizzy is looking better and better as she matures," said Holly. "We are regularly placed and have had some good placings at Championship shows."

Holly is now one of the top handlers in the UK; she has won her handling class at Crufts twice, and is regularly in the top three in the line-up.

Numbers went up again in the Barrington home when Kizzy produced a litter, and they kept a bitch, McHolglyn Cotton Candy, known as Darcy, who is now showing considerable promise in the ring. However, showing is just one of the activities that Holly does with her Westies.

GOOD CITIZENS

"I was very keen that my dogs learnt basic obedience, so we joined a general dog training class. All my dogs worked through the Good Citizen award scheme, and they all gained their gold awards very quickly. They enjoyed working in obedience and doing tricks so much, we felt that it was a shame to stop. So we decided that we would start doing obedience competitively, and the dogs have thoroughly enjoyed it. Westies are a really intelligent breed and are very willing to please."

Holly joined the Young Kennel Club (YKC), and qualified to compete in Obedience at Crufts with Kizzy by winning first place in a YKC qualifying class, which is open to all breeds and all ages of dogs.

"Kizzy had worked so hard and really deserved that first place," said Holly. "It was amazing, but I was really nervous when we walked into the big ring at Crufts. It was Kizzy who helped me to get over my nerves, as she is such a steady dog and nothing fazes her. We were in a huge class with over 30 entries and we came fourth, which was a huge achievement."

Holly is now regularly placed with Kizzy, and is working Graduate in YKC Obedience and Beginners/Novice in Obedience (all ages). She has found that joining the YKC has opened many doors in the dog world.

"The YKC has been really helpful and I recommend it to all young competitors in any dog sport," said Holly. "As well as competing in handling, breed, and showing, Kizzy and I take part in heelwork to music and agility. I have many like-minded friends whom I have met at YKC Summer Camps – it is nice to have friends who understand the 'dog world'!"

Holly is one of the few handlers in the UK to have made her mark with Westies in a variety of disciplines. What does she particularly like about the Westie character?

UNIQUE CHARACTER

"The Westie is a little dog with a huge personality," said Holly. "We are convinced that our Westies think that they are Great Danes, as they have all the attitude of a big dog. We are an active family and they fit in perfectly to our lifestyle. I can do agility, heelwork to music, show

Holly pictured in the show ring with Kizzy (Cabon Sea Maiden at McHolglyn).

them, work them in obedience, but they are quite happy to curl up with us, watching TV, and to walk miles with us the next day.

"The Breed Standard refers to West Highland White Terriers as being 'feisty', and they certainly are. But they are very easy characters to live with.

Continued on page 116...

Continued from page 115...

All Westies are different; you can't predict a character based on other Westies. For example, Kizzy is very relaxed and is never fazed by anything, whereas her daughter is very attached to us and can be a bit of a hooligan at times.

"When it comes to training, they can be quite stubborn at times and they take a bit longer than some breeds to learn things. But they are also very intelligent, and my youngster, Darcy, is the fastest-moving dog I've ever worked with. She behaves exactly like a collie, trying to pre-empt commands and trying to work me!"

"I personally find it easier to train my girls, as my boy is still entire and being a Westie he gets distracted and would rather investigate interesting smells or other things than concentrate on stays!"

According to Holly, the key to training a Westie, and indeed any dog, is motivation.

MOTIVATION

"I have helped to train many different breeds, and, as long as you can find something that the dog is really keen to work for, then the dog is willing and will enjoy working," she said. "For example, Bertie is really motivated by squeaky toys, whereas Darcy will work purely for praise and a game at the end. Most dogs are food motivated, but even then you have to find the dog's favourite type of food. Training dogs is all about knowing what will work best for your particular dog."

Holly has a brilliant rapport with Kizzy (Cabon Sea Maiden at McHolglyn) and they have a real working partnership.

Over the years, Holly has built up the special skills needed to work with little dogs.

"When you are training a little dog, such as a Westie, it is important to adapt the standard training techniques," she said. "For example, when teaching heelwork, little dogs tend to go wide of your body so that they can see your face. It is therefore advisable to use a touch stick, or teach them to target touch their face against your leg, so that they achieve the correct obedience heelwork position. This also applies to teaching smaller dogs to do a close and tight 'present' after a recall or a retrieve. I teach the correct position by sitting down at the dog's level, and I only progress to standing up when they have fully understood what is required. This is because little dogs like to look at your face and your eyes to understand what is expected of them."

SENSE OF HUMOUR
Competing with a Westie does not always go according to plan – and that is when a sense of humour becomes essential.

"I will never forget my first obedience show with Bertie, on the Isle of Anglesey," said Holly. "We were doing quite well, and Bertie, who is a very happy, bubbly character, had concentrated all of the way round. However, when it came to the stays, we were in a ring next to a field of sheep. Thinking that it was best to place Bertie with his back to the sheep, I positioned him at the far side of the ring. Every so often he would turn around and have a sneaky glance at the sheep, but he didn't break his sit-stay and was trying his best to focus on the task in hand.

"But just as we were in the middle of the stays, the sheep broke the fence and they all came running into the ring. At that point, Bertie was up and, in true Westie style, was after them, trying his best to be a collie and round them all up! As you can imagine, we didn't get placed – in fact, we got

Holly pictured with Darcy (left) and Kizzy (right).

eliminated – but I think Bertie had fun!"

Holly loves all the disciplines she competes in – but it is handling where she feels that her special bond with Kizzy comes to the fore.

"I love obedience and agility, and the dogs love learning new tricks, but I have a particular passion for handling," she said. "It's an activity where I feel that Kizzy and I are working completely in unison; she knows exactly what to do and is my rock in the ring. I couldn't imagine working with a dog that is more aware of what is required of her."

THE PERFECT WEST HIGHLAND WHITE TERRIER

Chapter 7

The 'perfect' West Highland White Terrier is the dog that conforms most closely to the Breed Standard. But what is the Breed Standard, I hear you wondering?

Well, each breed that is recognised by the Kennel Club is issued with a Breed Standard. This Standard is a blueprint for each breed, and is used to guide breeders and judges in the correct points for that particular breed. The Breed Standard we know today for the West Highland White Terrier has altered very little from the time it was first set out and recognised by the Kennel Club in about 1908.

For anyone intending to breed West Highlands, whether for the occasional litter for pleasure or for more serious breeding, with sights set on the summit of success, which means producing at least one Champion or more, then the Standard must be studied until it is well known by heart. However, this should not be a casual study; the Standard should be known so well that any particular point leaps to mind. It may be difficult to breed the perfect Westie, but a breeder should know instinctively what he/she is trying to achieve. Bear in mind, it costs no more to rear a prospective Champion than some ill-begotten pup with every imaginable fault – and there is great deal more pleasure in looking at the correct result.

Always remember, the West Highland is a working terrier, and he had to be as tough as the rocks of his native land. His name indicates what is expected of the breed: a dog that is hardy, tough and game, intelligent, cheerful and independent – and always ready to do a day's work. From the earliest days, the West Highland was prized for his ability to kill rats, to hunt and kill badgers, and to dig and squeeze his way into almost inaccessible places. So it is important to know what sort of ribs a dog should have to achieve this, and why so small a dog has such muscle and strength. These days, it is unlikely that a West Highland would ever get the chance to use his hunting skills. But he should still come close to the ideal laid down in the Breed Standard, so in theory, he could still do the job he was bred for.

Overseas, the American Kennel Club and the FCI (the European Kennel Club) also issue their own Breed Standards. The FCI models its Standards on the Standard used in a breed's country of origins, and therefore there is little difference between the FCI and the KC Standards. The AKC Standard is worded differently and is therefore open to a slightly different interpretation in some areas.

The West Highland is a tough, hardy terrier, and even though his hunting skills may not be required, he should appear capable of carrying out a day's work.

ANALYSIS AND INTERPRETATION

GENERAL APPEARANCE

KC
Strongly built; deep in chest and back ribs; level back and powerful quarters on muscular legs and exhibiting in a marked degree a great combination of strength and activity.

AKC
The West Highland White Terrier is a small, game, well-balanced hardy looking terrier, exhibiting good showmanship, possessed with no small amount of self-esteem, strongly built, deep in chest and back ribs, with a straight back and powerful hindquarters on muscular legs, and exhibiting in marked degree a great combination of strength and activity. The coat is about two inches long, white in color, hard, with plenty of soft undercoat. The dog should be neatly presented, the longer coat on the back and sides, trimmed to blend into the shorter neck and shoulder coat. Considerable hair is left around the head to act as a frame for the face to yield a typical Westie expression.

Both the KC and the AKC Breed Standards begin in the same way with the general appearance and characteristics; an overview, if you like. We should always have in our minds what the breed was designed for. Of course, he is a terrier. The word 'terra' comes from the latin word 'earth'. So we have a dog designed to go to earth; one that could go underground and flush out badgers, foxes etc. It is said that the West Highland White was originally the white offspring of the Cairn Terrier, which is why you often see a creamy line along a Westie's back. How true this really is I'm not sure, but it is what we are led to believe by the history books.

Because the breed was designed to go to ground then he had to have shorter legs. Long

Ch. Krisma Streetwise: The British Breed Standard calls for a strongly built dog, showing a combination of strength and activity.

Ch. Dawn's Maid N' America: Dam of 10 Champions, owned and bred by Dawn Martin. The convention in the USA is to exhibit a dog that is far more highly presented than the more natural-looking terrier shown in the UK.

legs and he would probably get stuck down a hole! He was white because he could be seen more easily and his double coat was water resistant and the undercoat would keep him warm on the Scottish moors.

CHARACTERISTICS AND TEMPERAMENT

KC
Small, active, game, hardy, possessed of no small amount of self-esteem with a varminty appearance.
Alert, gay, courageous, self-reliant but friendly.

AKC
Alert, gay, courageous and self-reliant, but friendly. Faults– Excess timidity or excess pugnacity.

Both these descriptions are fairly easy to understand except the last part in the KC Standard which refers to 'varminty' appearance. The English dictionary gives it as 'troublesome', I would like to think of it as 'get up and go'.

I believe that both the KC Standard and the AKC Standard fail to emphasise the character, adaptability and all-round purpose of this versatile breed. The West Highland is the best tempered of all the terrier breeds; he is a game and energetic worker, yet able to adapt with ease to the artificial life of a city

dweller. With his distinctive white coat, black nose and varminty expression, he will always be noticed and stand out in a crowd.

HEAD AND SKULL

KC
Skull slightly domed; when handled across forehead presents a smooth contour. Tapering very slightly from skull at level of ears to eyes. Distance from occiput to eyes slightly greater than length of foreface. Head thickly coated with hair, and carried at right angle or less, to axis of neck. Head not to be carried in extended position. Foreface gradually

The skull is broad, and is slightly domed between the ears.

tapering from eye to muzzle. Distinct stop formed by heavy, bony ridges immediately above and slightly overhanging eye, and slight indentation between eyes. Foreface not dished nor falling away quickly below eyes, where it is well made up. Jaws strong and level. Nose black and fairly large, forming smooth contour with rest of muzzle. Nose not projecting forward.

Eyes: Set wide apart, medium in size, not full, as dark as possible. Slightly sunk in head, sharp and intelligent, which,

looking from under heavy eyebrows, impart a piercing look. Light coloured eyes highly undesirable.

Ears: Small, erect and carried firmly, terminating in sharp point, set neither too wide nor too close. Hair short and smooth (velvety), should not be cut. Free from any fringe at top. Round-pointed, broad, large or thick ears or too heavily coated with hair most undesirable.

Mouth: As broad between canine teeth as is consistent with varminty expression required. Teeth large for large

size of dog, with regular scissor bite, i.e. upper teeth closely overlapping lower teeth and set square to the jaws.

AKC
Head: Shaped to present a round appearance from the front. Should be in proportion to the body.

Expression: Piercing, inquisitive, pert.

Eyes: Widely set apart, medium in size, almond shaped, dark brown in color, deep set, sharp and intelligent. Looking from under heavy eyebrows, they give a piercing look. Eye rims are black. Faults – Small, full or light colored eyes.

Ears: Small, carried tightly erect, set wide apart, on the top outer edge of the skull. They terminate in a sharp point, and must never be cropped. The hair on the ears is trimmed short and is smooth and velvety, free of fringe at the tips. Black skin pigmentation is preferred. Faults – Round-pointed, broad, large, ears set closely together, not held tightly erect, or placed too low on the side of the head.

Skull: Broad, slightly longer than the muzzle, not flat on top but slightly domed between the ears. It gradually tapers to the eyes. There is a defined stop, eyebrows are heavy. Faults – Long or narrow skull.

Muzzle: Blunt, slightly shorter than the skull, powerful and gradually tapering to the nose, which is large and black. The jaws are level and powerful. Lip

pigment is black. Faults –
Muzzle longer than skull. Nose
color other than black.
Bite: The teeth are large for the
size of the dog. There must be
six incisor teeth between the
canines of both lower and
upper jaws. An occasional
missing premolar is acceptable.
A tight scissors bite with upper
incisors slightly overlapping the
lower incisors or level mouth is
equally acceptable. Faults –
Teeth defective or misaligned.
Any incisors missing or several
premolars missing. Teeth
overshot or undershot.

A West Highland's head is
extremely important, as it sets
him apart from other breeds. To
examine the head in more detail,
I would suggest you use both
hands. Place your hands at each
side of the head, behind the ears
and under the jaw bones. The
dog is now looking directly at
you. Because the head is heavily
furnished, examination has to be
done with your hands. If you run
your thumb from his nose
backwards to the point between
his eyes, this is where the stop
should be – and your thumb
should 'stop'! The stop is vital if
the head is to look right.

The Standard calls for 'heavy
boney ridges immediately above
and slightly over-hanging eye'. So
when you have run your thumb
to the stop, then move your
thumb to either side and over
the eyes. This is where the boney
ridge should be. When the eye is
under this ridge, it gives the
Westie his unique expression

Top-winning Ch. Olac Moonpilot, showing the typical piercing expression of the West Highland White Terrier.

that is so desirable.

A good, dark, well-shaped eye
of medium size is important; we
are looking for an almond shaped
eye, with black eye-rims, and the
very dark eye colour that gives
the the typical piercing
expression. A light-coloured eye
is undesirable; it is out of keeping
and spoils the characteristic
charm of the true Westie. You do
not want a 'cutey pie' look. This
may look sweet, but it is not
correct, no matter how attractive
it may be. This look usually
comes from the lack of stop and
boney ridge, and the wrong

shaped eye. Remember, this is a
working terrier; his eyes are set in
this way to protect them from the
quarry. In my experience, the
'chocolate box' look that is often
seen also comes with a softer
coat, which would be totally
useless in a working dog.

The nose should always be
black and fairly large.
Occasionally, a nose will fade in
the winter time, but this is
usually just a passing phase and
the correct pigmentation will
return in sunny weather.

The descriptions for the ears
are self-explanatory. Again, the

The teeth should meet in a scissor bite with the teeth of the upper jaw closely overlapping the teeth on the lower jaw.

need for small ears stems from working requirements; large ears could easily be torn by bracken or even the vermin itself. The AKC and the FCI Standards give faults for each section, and both state for ears: "Round pointed, broad, large, ears set too closely together, not held tightly erect or placed too low on the side of the head are to be faulted." Ears are also vital to the correct expression. A dog with an alert expression shows the real terrier character, and especially so when listening in an inquisitive way.

It is important that the muzzle is not thin or snipey. The Westie should have a strong foreface because he needs to have room

in the jaw bone to contain large, strong teeth that have the power to kill a large rat.

The mouth must be a regular scissor bite: the upper teeth folding over the bottom teeth, and the teeth set squarely in the jaw. The AKC Standard is more descriptive in that it states: "an occasional missing pre-molar (these are the small teeth set in the side of the jaw) is acceptable, but there must be six incisors in both the upper and lower jaws" and they will also accept a level bite.

NECK

KC

Sufficiently long to allow proper set on of head required, muscular and gradually thickening towards base allowing neck to merge into nicely sloping shoulders.

AKC

Muscular and well set on sloping shoulders. The length of neck should be in proportion to the remainder of the dog. Faults – Neck too long or too short.

The neck must be sufficiently long to allow proper set of head required. The AKC adds more detail stating the neck should be in proportion to the remainder of the dog. Here again the 'in proportion' expression comes into play. If a West Highland had a 'swan-like' neck then he would look out of balance. But nature looks after its own: if a dog had

too short a back and too long a neck, he would topple forward!

FOREQUARTERS

KC

Shoulders sloping backwards. Shoulder blades broad and lying close to chest wall. Shoulder joint placed forward, elbows well in, allowing foreleg to move freely, parallel to axis of body. Forelegs short and muscular, straight and thickly covered with short, hard hair.

AKC

Angulation, Shoulders: **Shoulder blades are well laid back and well knit at the backbone. The shoulder blade should attach to an upper arm of moderate length, and sufficient angle to allow for definite body overhang. Faults – Steep or loaded shoulders. Upper arm too short or too straight.**
Legs: **Forelegs are muscular and well boned. relatively short, but with sufficient length to set the dog up so as not to be too close to the ground. The legs are reasonably straight, and thickly covered with short hard hair. They are set in under the shoulder blades with definite body overhang before them. Height from elbow to withers and elbow to ground should be approximately the same. Faults – Out at elbows. Light bone, fiddle-front.**

The shoulders are a part of a dog's anatomy that seem to confuse a lot of people. I feel they should be understood, as they are a very important part of a dog's construction. If you run your hands from the neck backwards, you should stop at the correct shoulder placement. The shoulders should slope backwards and the shoulder blades should be broad and lie close to the chest wall. The shoulder joint should be placed forward and the elbow well tucked in, to allow the foreleg to move freely, on a parallel axis of body.

The forelegs are short and muscular, straight and thickly covered with short, hard hair. The neck should merge smoothly into the shoulders, which it will do if the shoulders have the correct layback – this is most important.

The body is compact with a flat, level topline.

The forelegs are short, straight and muscular.

Together with good shoulder placement, there will be the long, free stride, which really covers the ground and is such a joy to watch.

Many years ago, I remember someone describing how shoulders should look to the eye and was told they should resemble the neck of a champagne bottle and not that of a beer bottle! The front end, that is shoulders and front, should be more refined than the hindquarters that have the strength and power to allow the dog to move forward with a thrusting action.

The AKC Standard gives as its list of faults: "Steep or loaded (heavy) shoulders. Upper arm too short or too straight". The British Standard does not mention the upper arm – quite why this is, I do not know, as this can be such an important part of a shoulder construction. Run your hand up

the dog's leg and you will come to the bone that we refer to as the upper arm. It is this part that determines how much reach in front a dog has. If it is short and steep then you will get a high-stepping dog, or a dog moving with little forward reach.

BODY

KC

Compact. Back level, loins broad and strong. Chest deep and ribs well arched in upper half presenting a flattish side appearance. Back ribs of considerable depth and distance from last rib of quarters as short as compatible with free movement of body.

AKC

Topline: **Flat and level, both standing and moving. Faults – High rear, any deviation from above.**

Body: Compact and of good substance. Ribs deep and well arched in the upper half of rib, extending at least to the elbows, and presenting a flattish side appearance. Back ribs of considerable depth, and distance from last rib to upper thigh as short as compatible with free movement of the body. Chest very deep and extending to the elbows, with breadth in proportion to the size of the dog. Loin short, broad and strong. *Faults:* Back weak, either too long or too short. Barrel ribs, ribs above elbows.

HINDQUARTERS

KC
Strong, muscular and wide across top. Legs short, muscular and sinewy. Thighs very

The hindquarters are strong and muscular, providing the drive when a dog is moving.

muscular and not too wide apart. Hocks bent and well set in under body so as to be fairly close to each other when standing or moving. Straight or weak hocks most undesirable.

AKC
Angulation – Thighs are very muscular, well angulated, not set wide apart, with hock well bent, short, and parallel when viewed from the rear.
Legs – Rear legs are muscular and relatively short and sinewy.
Faults – Weak hocks, long hocks, lack of angulation. Cowhocks.

The hindquarters on a West Highland White are very important and this is where the drive comes from. A Westie pushes off from behind and so short hocks are required; long hocks would not enable the dog to push itself forward. The description of hocks being fairly close to each other when the dog is moving needs clarification. The hocks should not touch, but they will converge towards each other when the dog is moving.

A good bend of stifle is needed. Again, this is required for the drive that is so essential in the breed.

The AKC Standard lists among its faults: weak hocks, long hocks, lack of angulation, and cowhocks.

FEET

KC
Forefeet larger than hind, round, proportionate in size,

strong, thickly padded and covered with short harsh hair. Hindfeet are smaller and thickly padded. Under surface of pads and all nails preferably black.

AKC
Forefeet are larger than the hind ones, are round, proportionate in size, strong, thickly padded; they may properly be turned out slightly. Dewclaws may be removed. Black pigmentation is most desirable on pads of all feet and nails, although nails may lose coloration in older dogs. Hind feet are smaller than front feet, and are thickly padded. Dewclaws may be removed.

The reason why the feet front feet are larger than the hind ones goes back to the breed's working abilities. The front feet would be used for digging out the fox hole, and they needed to be well padded to give protection over the hard terrain a dog would cover. You never want to see splayed or open feet, as they do not fit in with the picture of a game, hardy terrier that can do a hard day's work on rough ground. The under surface of the pads and all the nails should be preferably black. The American Standard adds: "Dewclaws may be removed and feet may be properly turned out slightly".

TAIL

KC
13-15 cms (5-6 ins) long, covered with harsh hair, no

GAIT AND MOVEMENT

The West Highland's movement is free and straight, with drive coming from the hindquarters and the front legs extending forward from the shoulder.

feathering, as straight as possible, carried jauntily, not gay or carried over back. A long tail undesirable, and on no account should tails be docked.

AKC

Relatively short, with good substance, and shaped like a carrot. When standing erect it is never extended above the top of the skull. It is covered with hard hair without feather, as straight as possible, carried gaily but not curled over the back. The tail is set on high enough so that the spine does not slope down to it. The tail is never docked. Faults – Set too low, long, thin, carried at half-mast, or curled over back.

When I started in the breed I was always told you wanted a tail resembling a carrot! The West Highland's tail should be thick at the root and tapering to a point. I believe the size of the tail depends on the individual dog. When a West Highland is standing alert, the tail should be no higher than the top of his head. A long tail is undesirable and on no account, should tails be docked. A short tail is required because if a dog went into a hole or similar, then the owner could grab hold of the tail and pull him out.

GAIT/MOVEMENT

KC

Free, straight and easy all round. In front, legs freely extended forward from shoulder. Hind movement free, strong and close. Stifle and hocks well flexed and hocks drawn under body giving drive. Stiff, stilted movement behind and cowhocks highly undesirable.

AKC

Free, straight and easy all around. It is a distinctive gait, not stilted, but powerful, with reach and drive. In front the leg is freely extended forward by the shoulder. When seen from the front the legs do not move square, but tend to move toward the center of gravity. The hind movement is free, strong and fairly close. The hocks are freely flexed and drawn close under the body, so that when moving off the foot the body is thrown or pushed forward with some force. Overall ability to move is usually best evaluated from the side, and topline remains level. *Faults:* Lack of reach in front, and/or drive behind. Stiff, stilted or too wide movement.

The AKC Standard is more descriptive in this area, but it is basically the same as the English Standard.

COAT

KC
Double coated. Outer coat consists of harsh hair, about 5 cms (2 ins) long, free from any curl. Undercoat, which resembles fur, short, soft and close. Open coats most undesirable.

AKC
Very important and seldom seen to perfection. Must be double-coated. The head is shaped by plucking the hair, to present the round appearance. The outer coat consists of straight hard white hair, about two inches long, with shorter coat on neck and shoulders, properly blended and trimmed to blend shorter areas into furnishings, which are longer on stomach and legs. The ideal coat is hard, straight and white, but a hard straight coat which may have some wheaten tipping is preferable to a white fluffy or soft coat. Furnishings may be somewhat softer and longer but should never give the appearance of fluff. Faults – Soft coat. Any silkiness or tendency to curl. Any open or single coat, or one which is too short.

The West Highland has a double coat. The outer coat consists of harsh hair, about 5 cms (2 ins) long, and free from curl. The undercoat, which resembles fur, is short, soft and close. Open coats are most undesirable. For a working terrier, the coat is very important, as it gives protection when a dog is out on the moors in extreme weather conditions. The outer harder hair expels rain, and the softer undercoat keeps him warm. A soft, fluffy coat would be no help whatsoever in bad weather; it would absorb the wet and the dog would be cold in minutes. No matter how cute this soft coat may look, it is totally incorrect

COLOUR

KC
White.

AKC
The color is white, as defined by the breed's name. Faults – Any coat color other than white. Heavy wheaten color.

The coat, of course, is always white. Occasionally you get a little 'colour' on the middle of a West Highland's back; this would be a creamy, slightly red colour. This colour pops up now and again, usually occurring in dogs that have particularly hard coats. However if you go back into the early records, the interpretations on colour were a little different. In all the old records I have come across it was freely admitted that a sandy or yellowish streak down

It is every breeder's dream to make up a Champion. Jennie Griffith of the Karamynd kennel excelled, breeding three Champions in one litter. They are (left to right); Ch. Karamynd High As Kite, Ch. Karamynd Play To The Crowd, and Ch. Karamynd Paws For Applause.

the back was usually present and was permitted. Now the description means what it says, and a poor-coloured coat is penalised.

SIZE

KC
Height at withers approximately 28 cms (11 ins).

AKC
The ideal size is eleven inches at the withers for dogs and ten inches for bitches. A slight deviation is acceptable. The Westie is a compact dog, with good balance and substance. The body between the withers and the root of the tail is slightly shorter than the height at the withers. Short-coupled and well boned. *Faults:* **Over or under height limits. Fine boned.**

The approximate size for a West Highland White Terrier is 28 cms (11 ins); the AKC Standard states that males should be 11 ins (28 cms) and females 10 ins (25.5 cms). There was a most significant change made in 1948 at a joint meeting of the committees of the Scottish and English breed clubs, which was held in Edinburgh. It was agreed that the height should be about 11 ins at the shoulder, as against the previous 8-12 inches (20-30.5 cms) that had been the accepted height from the days of the original Standard. The weights of 14-18 lbs (6.3-8 kgs) for dogs and 12-16 lbs (5.5-7 kgs) for bitches were abandoned, and are

The judge's task is to look at the dog as a whole to find the correct, balanced picture which comes closest to the 'perfect' West Highland White Terrier.

therefore not included in the present Standard.

In his book, *The West Highland White Terrier*, written in 1911, Holland Buckley wrote that Brogach, the sire of Morven, was 17 lbs (7.7 kgs) in weight; Athol, Morven's best son, was 16 lbs (8 kgs) and Model, the great-grandson of Brogarth, was also 16 lbs. The West Highland should never appear like a Scottish Terrier with its low-slung heavy body and neither should it have the lightness of a Cairn Terrier. For weight and size, the West Highland should be in between both these breeds.

FAULTS

KC
Any departure from the foregoing points should be considered a fault and the seriousness with which the fault should be regarded should be in

exact proportion to its degree and its effect upon the health and welfare of the dog.
Note: Male animals should have two apparently normal testicles fully descended into the scrotum.

AKC
The faults are listed within the Breed Standard.

SUMMING UP
The Breed Standards are designed to guide those wishing to judge the breed, giving a clear picture of the West Highland White Terrier's requirements. However, you should never judge on just one part; you must assess the dog as a whole, and each part should fit together. When judging we are looking for a balanced dog, all parts fitting together, to achieve the picture we have in our minds of a perfect West Highland White Terrier.

HAPPY AND HEALTHY

Most terriers enjoy life if they are healthy and given plenty of exercise. Your West Highland White will rely on you to provide him with all that he requires – suitable food, health care, exercise and a good home with necessary parasite control.

Visits to the veterinary surgeon will be required for vaccinations, at which time it is usual to make a physical examination of the dog for any undisclosed disease. In between times, daily grooming provides the opportunity to get to know the dog's body structure and coat, so that signs of illness can be detected earlier than if left until the dog is in pain or refusing food. The introduction of balanced and improved diets, along with routine vaccinations, are contributing to a much longer lifespan for all domestic

animals, but the owner of the dog also has a role to play in everyday health care.

It is very important that you really get to know your dog, as it will help you to identify when he is 'off colour'. You should then be able to decide whether the dog needs rest or to be taken to the veterinary surgery. It is also important to know the signs of a healthy dog when you go to buy a puppy. Visits to the vet should be made soon after acquiring a Westie when any abnormality may be detected.

Pet insurance cover has provided the opportunity for extensive tests and procedures to be undertaken on dogs. You should always find out what each policy will offer and if there are limits put on the total claim expense, age limit or hereditary disorders requiring veterinary attention before buying insurance.

VACCINATIONS

It is best to take all available measures to keep your Westie healthy; one of the greatest advances in canine practice in the last 50 years has been the development of effective vaccines to prevent disease. Within living memory dogs died from fits after distemper virus infections and in the last 20 years many puppies have contracted parvovirus, which, in the early years, often proved to be fatal. The routine use of a multiple component vaccine to protect against canine distemper, infectious canine hepatitis, parvovirus and Leptospirosis is accepted, but there are still local differences in the age the puppy receives his first injection or 'shot'. The timing for the primary vaccine course doses is based on an understanding of when the immunity provided by the mother declines to a level that will not interfere with the immune response. Canine vaccines currently in use in the UK have recommendations for the final dose of the primary course to be given at 10 or 12 weeks of age; and booster injections after the first year are usual. The length of protection provided after two injections against Leptospirosis given to a puppy is not significantly greater than 12 months (challenges after this date results in shedding of leptospires), and for some vaccines it is considered less than 12 months. For the protection against the dog viruses, a minimum of three years is possible and here annual boosters are less essential. In the way of natural things, not all dogs would be protected after their first dose, so further booster vaccination is recommended at intervals, as decided by the vet with a local knowledge, so as to protect any of those individual dogs who may have low or marginal blood level titres against fatal diseases.

Kennel cough is a distressing infectious disease usually acquired from airborne contact with other dogs, especially those stressed when visiting dog shows or boarding kennels. There are several vaccines available and advice should be obtained from the vet as to which type of protection is appropriate to your

Your vet will advise on the best age to start a vaccination programme.

dog's exposure. A rabies vaccine is necessary for all dogs leaving the United Kingdom, but is routine in many countries, as is the vaccine for Lyme disease in the USA, where it should be discussed with the veterinarian. Coronavirus as a cause of diarrhoea is not life-threatening and vaccination is not usually considered necessary.

WORMING & PARASITE CONTROL

Routine worming every three months is obligatory to reduce the risk of infection of susceptible humans handling the dog. De-wormers are necessary for puppies as well as for adult dogs. Many puppies are infested with

roundworms, but some breeders start worming the bitch during pregnancy to reduce the risk to the newborn pups. Worming the puppy from two weeks, repeated at regular intervals, is advised. Roundworms, hookworms, tapeworms and whipworms present different threats, while heartworms, which can result after the bite of an infected mosquito, are a particular problem in the south-east Atlantic and Gulf Coasts of the USA. This is another parasite to consider if you are planning to take your dog to mainland Europe, as heartworm is endemic from the Mediterranean area of France southwards.

Fleas are wingless insects that are a nuisance to pets; a single flea on the dog's coat can cause persistent scratching and restlessness. Even after the flea has been removed, the bites will cause skin disease, particularly if there is hypersensitivity to the flea antigen.

Fleas may also carry the larvae of the worm Dipylidium, which causes tapeworms to develop in the host's intestine when the flea is swallowed by a dog, cat or even a child. Many effective anti-flea preparations are now available – some as tablets by mouth, some as coat applications and some as residual sprays to apply to carpets and upholstery frequented by cats as well as dogs.

Puppies are routinely treated for roundworm.

Lice, fleas, Cheyletiella, and some other mites that burrow under the skin may all cause disease and are not easily recognised by the eye. Ticks are seen when they become large and visible as they gorge themselves with the dog's blood. A thorough grooming of the dog each day will detect many of these parasites; apply suitable preventive products as needed. These may be supplied as a powder, a shampoo, a spot-on insecticide or spray.

DIET AND EXERCISE

Many West Highland White Terriers are naturally lean and although they may look as though they are underweight, they are perfectly fit. It is a good idea to weigh all dogs on a regular basis; the dog that appears thin, but still actively fit, has fewer reserves to fall back on, and weighing on a weekly basis can detect further weight loss before any disastrous changes can occur. Each dog should have an ideal weight and within a narrow range the actual correct weight for the dog will act as a guide.

Obesity has become a major concern for dogs as well as humans, and appetite suppressants for dogs can now be used. Mitratapide (Yarvitan), available from the vet, can be used as part of an overall weight management programme.

COAT, EARS AND FEET

Too much confinement indoors with warm room temperatures can lead to the loss of undercoat and less hair density for outdoor protection. The Westie may shed hair like other dogs, but, being white, it shows up more on carpets and furniture. Regular brushing will keep the shedding to a minimum.

Grooming stimulates the hair growth stage known as anagen by the removal of dead, shedding hairs. This helps to prevent bareness or bald patches. The removal of any eye or other discharge prevents coat matting and skin irritation. The close inspection of the animal during grooming assists in early recognition of problems. During grooming, take care to examine any bony prominences, skin folds, feet and claws, eyes and ears, mouth and teeth, anus, vulva and prepuce.

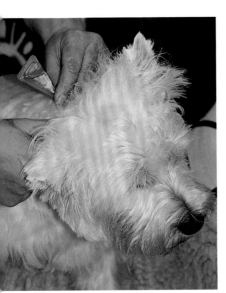

Spot-on treatment is effective in the prevention of external parasites.

These regular checks for traces of fleas or ticks attached to the skin can prevent itching and hair loss. When grooming the dog, always make a point of checking the ears both inside and out. There may often be a slightly sweet smell, but as soon as ear problems occur, the aroma becomes very pungent. The start of ear trouble can also be detected by the way the dog holds his head. You may need to wash the West Highland White, either to eradicate and control ectoparasites or to cleanse the coat and remove smells. Bathing is often used to improve the appearance of the coat before a show.

The pads of the feet should feel quite soft to the touch and not leathery or horny (hyperkeratinised). The skin between the toes is very sensitive to chemical burns, and some alkaline clay soils will provoke inflammation with lameness, known as 'pedal eczema'. The nails should be of even length and not split at the ends after being left to grow too long. If the nails are too long, they will have to be clipped, being especially careful to avoid hurting the dog by cutting into the quick. Exercise on hard concrete surfaces and pavements is normally sufficient to keep nails at reasonable length; tarmac roads and tarred pavements often do not provide enough friction to wear down nails. Dewclaws, if present, are not a disadvantage to the dog, but, if they should grow in a circle, they can penetrate the flesh, causing an infected wound.

A TO Z OF COMMON AILMENTS

ALLERGIES
A now frequent diagnosis for many dog skin and intestinal disorders, it is the result of an inappropriate immune response by the dog to an antigen in the food or to one inhaled through the nose. Unfortunately, there are many antigens that can affect dogs and diagnostic skin and blood tests may not always identify the disease factor. A process of eliminating possible antigens in the diet or in the environment may help to find a cause and there are many commercial diets available that may help. Medication can be used to suppress the allergic response and both antihistamines and steroids may be tried before the best treatment is found.

ALOPECIA
Alopecia is the partial or complete absence of hair from areas of the skin where it is normally present; often a patchy coat loss is seen at first. This disorder is usually hormonal, associated with hypothyroidism, hyperadrenocorticism (Cushing's disease), Sertoli cell tumour of the testes, or, in females, an ovarian imbalance of the hormones. Hair loss may occur after animal bites, but when hair is absent from both sides of the body (often on the flanks) and the skin is neither itchy or inflamed, treatment must first be based on identifying and treating the underlying cause. Lotions applied direct to the skin will not provide a cure, but moisturising creams will reduce scaliness.

ANAL DISORDERS (ANAL SACCULITIS, TUMOURS: ADENOMATA)
Modern diets are often blamed for dogs needing their anal 'glands' squeezed out at regular intervals. These glands are actually little sacs just at the edge of the anus opening and contain strong-smelling, greasy substances used to 'mark' the freshly passed faeces for other animals to recognise. Over-production of the fluid causes the dog discomfort and when a suitable floor surface is available the dog will then 'scoot' along, leaving a trail of odorous matter.

Occasionally, infection alters the smell and may result in other dogs being attracted to a female-type odour; a course of antibiotics can have a direct effect on this apparent behaviour problem. Abscesses of the anal sacs are very painful. They may require drainage although often they swell and burst on their own with a sudden blood-stained discharge; flushing out and antibiotics may be required as treatment.

Other glands around the anus may become cancerous and attention is drawn to these when bleeding occurs. Adenomata are found in the older male dog and require veterinary attention before bleeding occurs.

ARTHRITIS

This is a joint disease that was once often found after an infection, but now it is usually either due to joint wear and tear (degenerative) or as a result of the immune system reaction: for example, rheumatoid arthritis and idiopathic arthritis. Treatment is aimed at keeping the dog mobile, excess weight should be lost, and anti-inflammatory medication administered daily will remove pain and discomfort.

ATOPY

Sometimes known as inhalant allergy atopy, it is associated with many chronic skin diseases characterised by pruritus – a sensation within the skin that provokes the Westie to have a desire to scratch, lick, chew or

Arthritis is more likely to affect the older dog.

rub itself to alleviate the irritation. It is more common in the Westie than in other breeds, and early attention and diagnosis may require specific tests and medication to relieve the condition. The signs do not usually develop until one to three years and include stained hair and roughened, itchy, oozing skin, caused by the immune reactions to various allergens (such as fleas or pollen). There is an indication of an inherited tendency, as some breeds are more susceptible.

BENIGN TUMOURS

Benign tumours are those cancers that are not invading the body aggressively, but appear as swellings or lumps often detected during the grooming process. They do not attack the body, but can cause problems if they grow large, such as a lipoma in the armpit (axilla), or are in such a position that they get knocked or bleed after scratching. Most warts are benign growths, but they have to be distinguished from 'mast cell tumours' that occur on the skin of the body, especially

A responsible owner should learn the principles of first-aid.

the lower abdomen and hind legs, and may be life-threatening. Growths may be present for months or years before suddenly enlarging. If you have any doubts, consult your vet; biopsy test should be taken on such tumours and surgical excision may be called for.

BONE FRACTURES
Most broken bones are the result of some avoidable injury, an old dog with kidney disease may have brittle bones, but spontaneous fractures are quite rare even then. Treatment of fractures will require the attention of the vet, but there is little point in attempting first aid, as the Westie will be in pain and will adopt the most comfortable position he can find. Natural painkillers known as endorphins

come into action immediately following such an injury. If there is a skin wound associated with the fracture, this should be covered to reduce bacterial contamination, lessening the risk of osteomyelitis before the break in the bone can be satisfactorily repaired. X-rays will be necessary to confirm a crack or a major displacement of bones.

BURNS & SCALDS
First-aid measures require immediate cooling of the skin by pouring cold water over the injury repeatedly for at least 10 minutes. Some scalds from spilt hot water or oil will penetrate the coat and may not be seen until a large area of skin and hair peels away, because heat has killed the surface skin cells. As these injuries are considered to be very

painful, analgesics (pain relief) should be obtained, and in anything but the smallest injured area, antibiotics should be administered, as secondary bacteria will multiply on exposed raw surfaces. Bandages and dressings are not a great help, but cling film has been used as an effective protective layer in some situations. Clipping the hair away over a large area surrounding the burn and then flushing the areas with saline can be helpful if tolerated by the dog. An Elizabethan collar can be used to prevent the Westie licking the area. In cases showing signs of shock, intravenous fluid therapy may be a necessity.

CALCULI
Stones were often thought to be the cause of a dog straining to pass urine and where these signs are shown a veterinary examination for bladder inflammation (cystitis) or tumours is advised. Calculi are deposits of mineral salts from the urine, either in the neck of the bladder or nearer the base of the penis in the male. Stones can also form in the kidneys where they cause pain as they enter the ureters, but the bladder is not affected.

Calculi are recognisable on X-ray or with ultrasound examinations. The obstruction may be partial when the dog or bitch spends an unusually long time passing urine, or in males sometimes no urine can be voided – the dog strains, looking uncomfortable or in pain. An operation is usually necessary to remove calculi and diet advice will be given on how to avoid further attacks. Increasing the dog's water intake and providing opportunities for frequent bladder emptying are important in prevention.

CANCER – CARCINOMA

Carcinoma may be seen as an abnormal swelling or 'growth', but internal tumours will not be recognised so readily. Bleeding from the mouth, nose or rectum should always arouse fears of a tumour. Skin tumours may be first noticed as sores that will not heal or raised areas with a tendency to bleed.

Sarcomas are malignant tumours arising from the connective tissues, one of the commonest forms is lymphosarcoma, a tumour of the lymph tissues. Mammary tumours are probably the most common cancers of the bitch, but are rarely found in females spayed before their second season. About 50 per cent of such tumours in the dog are benign, but mixed tumours may occur and removal of affected glands is usually advised. The earlier a tumour is found the better and the vet may need to X-ray or take cell samples known as biopsies. Treatment will depend on the result of such tests. Surgical excision may be the first treatment applied, but other tumours respond to chemotherapy or to radiotherapy. Freezing using cryotherapy is one of many treatments that may be

Advances in veterinary science mean that many more conditions can be treated with a successful outcome.

appropriate for a certain type of growth and the tumour appears to be completely removed. Palliative surgery may be used to remove a tumour to improve the animal's quality of life even though it does not alter the long-term prognosis.

CATARACTS

Any opaqueness of the lens of the eye is termed a cataract; the dog may become blind and the eye develops a pearl-like quality. Cataracts are most commonly seen in old age or dogs with diabetes, but they can occur in young dogs following an injury (such as a thorn piercing the eye). Westies are rarely are affected with congenital cataracts, which are seen once the puppy opens its eyes. Once a condition has been diagnosed, cataract

surgery performed at a specialised ophthalmic centre is very successful in suitably selected cases

COLLAPSE

Sudden collapse and possible loss of consciousness is associated with any sudden pain or possibly poisoning; if seen in old age, it is more likely to be due to heart or circulatory failure. Ensuring that the dog has a clear airway for breathing and massaging the chest area may be all that can be done until the dog gets to a vet where a full examination will be necessary.

CONJUNCTIVITIS

Conjunctivitis is common in dogs with prominent eyes and the signs of a red eye with a watery or crusty discharge are easy to

DIABETES

There are two sorts found in the dog. 'Sugar diabetes', known as DM (diabetes mellitus), is seen more frequently in the older bitch. Caused by a lack of insulin to regulate the level of glucose in the blood, the signs include increased thirst, passing large quantities of urine, eye cataracts and muscle weakness, and are seen with an increased appetite and weight loss as the dog attempts to satisfy the variations of his sugar levels. Diagnosis by urine and blood samples is followed by the injection of a suitable insulin subcutaneously once or more daily. Some types of endocrine disease such as diabetes may arise as a result of an immune-mediated destruction of glandular tissues.

Diabetes insipidus is related to the water control mechanism of the kidneys, and is uncommon in dogs.

recognise. Dust blown by the wind, chemicals and allergies cause eye irritation, but a sudden, acute, severe conjunctivitis may indicate the presence of a foreign body, such as a grass seed under the eyelids. Careful examination of the inner surfaces of both eyelids and the third eyelid is necessary to identify and remove foreign material. Another cause is the in-turning of the edge of the eyelid, known as entropion, which is sometimes inherited, and surgical correction may be required.

CONSTIPATION

If the Westie is known to have consumed large quantities of bone or fibrous matter, straining may indicate a foreign body stuck in the rectum, or, in the male dog, it may be due to an enlarged prostate gland. Medication with liquid paraffin and increasing the fluid intake is advised, but if the problem continues, the vet should visited.

CYSTITIS

Inflammation of the bladder is more common in the female and may first be noticed by the bitch straining frequently with only small quantities of urine passed each time. Bacteria reaching the bladder from outside the body is the usual cause, although bladder calculi are fairly common in both sexes and will cause cystitis. In all cases, the fluid intake should be reviewed since a good 'wash through' of the bladder will reduce the risk of bacteria and mineral particles irritating the bladder lining. Medication with antispasmodics and an appropriate antibiotic will be required.

DISTEMPER

Fortunately, this virus infection that at one time caused devastating illnesses is now rare. Routine vaccination has been very effective in preventing disease, but there is always the threat of a Westie acquiring the infection if there has been a breakdown in the immune system. Affected dogs develop a high temperature, cough, diarrhoea and a purulent eye discharge; then, after several weeks, illness complications may still set in with pneumonia or damage to the nervous system seen as paralysis or fits.

EPILEPSY & FITS

Seizures occur relatively commonly in dogs. They represent an acute and usually brief disturbance of normal electrical activity in the brain, but they can be distressing for both the patient and the owner. Most fits last only a short time (less than two minutes) and owners often telephone for veterinary advice once the seizure is over. Fits can sometimes occur close together, and it is best to have the dog examined by a veterinary surgeon as soon as practical, even after the seizure has stopped. Some fits are prolonged or very frequent, and these seizures may cause permanent brain damage. Once the fits have passed, the dog may seem dull or confused for several hours; medication is used to control fits, but long-term treatment may be needed.

GASTRO-ENTERITIS

Vomiting is relatively common in dogs and it can be a protective mechanism to try to prevent poisonous substances entering the body. Gastro-enteritis includes diarrhoea attacks as a similar process, to get rid of undesirable intestine contents by washing them out. The production of extra mucus and intestinal fluid, coupled with a rapid bowel evacuation movement, accounts for the large volumes of slimy faeces. These products of gastro-enteritis are objectionable: distressing to the dog and unpleasant for the owner, who may have to clean up afterwards. There are many causes, ranging from the simplest (of the dog needing worming) to the complex interaction of viruses and bacteria that can cause an infection to spread through a kennel of dogs. Dietary diarrhoea may occur after a sudden change in foodstuff; after scavenging or due to an allergy to a particular food substance or additive. Where the signs of gastro-enteritis last more than 48 hours, a vet should be prepared to take samples and other tests to look for diseases such as pancreatitis, colitis or tumours among many other causes, since some disorders may be life-threatening.

Treatment at home may be tried using the principle of 'bowel rest': stopping feeding for 48 to 72 hours and allowing fluids in repeated small quantities. Ice cubes in place of water in the bowl may help reduce vomiting.

From weaning onwards, a Westie must be fed a good-quality diet.

Electrolyte solutions, as used in 'Travellers' Diarrhoea', help with rehydration. Once signs are alleviated, small feeds of smooth foods (such as steamed fish or chicken and boiled rice) may be gradually introduced. Where there is continual diarrhoea for three to four weeks, the disease is unlikely to be resolved without identifying a specific cause and using appropriate treatment.

HEARTWORM DISEASE

Heartworms are still uncommon in the UK, but they are a major problem in the USA where they are spread by mosquitoes. Dogs can be protected from six to eight weeks of age with a monthly dose of the medication advised by the veterinarian (there are a number of suitable products available). A blood test can be used to see if the heartworm antigen is present before commencing treatment and it can be repeated annually. The filarial worms live in the heart and blood vessels of the lungs and cause signs such as

Kennel cough can spread very rapidly in a situation such as a show when a lot of dogs are in close proximity.

tiring, intolerance of exercise and a soft, deep cough.

HEPATITIS
Inflammation of the liver may be due to a virus, but it is uncommon in dogs when they have been protected with the vaccines that also prevent the bacteria Leptospira from damaging the liver. Chronic liver disease may be due to heart failure, tumours or some type of toxicity; dietary treatment may help if there are no specific medicines to use.

JAUNDICE
The yellow colour of the skin, most noticeably seen in the white of the eye, is a sign of some liver damage and retention of the yellow pigment from the breakdown of blood haemoglobin. Jaundice is usually accompanied by a loss of appetite and general disinterest in going for walks, since the liver is a key

organ in the dog's body system controls. Veterinary attention is urgent, since with adequate treatment the jaundice will disappear over a few weeks; care must be taken to avoid further liver damage and some dogs may become carriers of infection.

KENNEL COUGH
The signs of a goose-honking cough, hacking or retching that lasts for days to several weeks is due to cell damage at the base of the windpipe and bronchial tubes. The dry and unproductive cough is caused by a combination of viruses, bacteria and mycoplasma. Vaccination is helpful in preventing the disease but may not give full protection, as strains of kennel cough seem to vary. The disease is highly contagious and spread by droplets, so it may be acquired at dog shows or boarding kennels. An incubation period of five to seven days is usual. Veterinary

treatments alleviate the cough and reduce the duration of the illness.

LEPTOSPIROSIS
Dogs that work in the country or swim in water are more likely to meet this infection. Leptospira bacteria carried by rats is found in pools and ditches where rodents have visited. Annual vaccination against the two types of Leptospira is advised. Treatment in the early stages using antibiotics is effective, but liver and kidney damage may permanently incapacitate the Westie if the early signs with a fever are not recognised. Kidney and liver failure may lead to death. Treatment with antibiotics for two to three weeks is needed to prevent the dog carrying Leptospira and infecting others.

LYME DISEASE BORRELIOSIS
This tick-borne disease affecting dogs, humans and, to a lesser

extent, other domestic animals is common in the USA; it is estimated that there may be a thousand cases a year in the UK. It often presents itself as a sudden lameness with a fever, or, in the chronic form, one or two joints are affected with arthritis, often the carpus (wrist joint), that alerts the Westie owner to this disease. Exposure to ticks (Ixodes ricinus in Britain) should raise suspicions if similar signs develop with swelling of a joint and loss of appetite, especially if a rash develops at the bite, which soon spreads. Treatment is effective, and blood tests can be used to confirm Borrelia at the laboratory.

MANGE MITES

Several types affecting dogs are recognised and may be the cause of scratching, hair loss and ear disease. Sarcoptic mange causes the most irritation and is diagnosed by skin scrapings or a blood test. Demodectic mange is less of a problem and is diagnosed by skin scrapes or from plucked hairs. Otodectic mange occurs in the ears and the mite can be found in the wax. Cheyletiella is a surface mite of the coat; it causes white 'dandruff' signs and is diagnosed by coat brushing or sellotape impressions for microscope inspection. These mite infections first need identifying, but can then be treated with acaracide medication provided by the vet. Older traditional treatments required frequent bathing of the dog. Repeat treatments after 10 to 14 days are needed to prevent reinfestation.

NEPHRITIS

Dogs may suffer acute kidney failure after poisoning, obstructions to the bladder or after shock with reduced blood supply. Chronic nephritis is more common in older dogs, where the blood accumulates waste products that the damaged kidneys cannot remove. The nephritic syndrome is caused by an immune-mediated damage within the kidney. The signs of increased thirst, loss of appetite and progressive weight loss are commonly seen in kidney disease.

OTITIS EXTERNA

Ear diseases are more common in terriers such as Westies that have standing-up ears. When there is a lot of hair around the ear, the ventilation of the tube to the ear drum is poor and may encourage bacteria to multiply. When otitis occurs, a strong-smelling discharge develops and the dog shakes his head or may show a head tilt. The presence of a grass seed in the ear canal should always be suspected in dogs that have been out in long grass in the summer months; after becoming trapped by the hair, the seed can quickly work its way down the ear canal and can even penetrate the ear drum. The spikes of the grass seed prevent it being shaken out of the ear and veterinary extraction of the seed is essential.

A West Highland has a lot of hair around the ears, and this may result in poor ventilation of the tube leading to the ear drum.

PARVOVIRUS

This virus infection, commonly seen in younger dogs, is most dangerous to the recently weaned puppy. Vaccination schedules are devised to protect susceptible dogs and the vet should be asked as to when and how often a parvo vaccine should be used in your locality. The virus has an incubation of about three to five days. It attacks the bowels with a sudden onset of vomiting and diarrhoea. Blood may be passed, dehydration sets in and sudden death is possible. Isolation from other puppies is essential and the replacement of the fluids and electrolytes lost is urgent. Medication to stop the vomiting, antibiotics against secondary bacteria, and later a smooth, bland diet should be provided.

PARALYSIS & INTERVERTEBRAL DISC DISEASE

Collapse or sudden weakness of the hindquarters may be due to pressure on the nerves of the spine that supply the muscles and other sensory receptors. The 'slipped disc', as it is commonly known, may be responsible, but any injury to the spine (a fibrocartilage embolism, a fracture or a tumour) may cause similar paralysis. The signs are similar, with dragging one or both hind legs, lack of tail use and often the loss of bladder and bowel control. X-rays, a neurological assessment and possibly an MRI scan will be needed to be certain of the cause. Some cases respond well to surgical correction but others can be treated medically, which may be effective and is less costly. Home nursing care should include keeping the dog clean and groomed, helping with bladder or bowel movements, and carrying out any physiotherapy advised by the veterinary surgeon. Sudden movements in the case of spinal fractures must be avoided when carrying a patient with any back injury.

PROSTATE DISEASE

Elderly dogs that have not been castrated may show signs of straining, which may be thought to be a sign of constipation, but the real cause is often an enlarged prostate gland at the neck of the bladder. Most often it is a benign enlargement that causes pressure into the rectum, rather than blocking the bladder exit. Once diagnosed, hormone injections, combined with a laxative diet, are very effective.

PYOMETRA

At one time pyometra was the commonest cause of illness in middle-aged to elderly bitches; the disease of the uterus would be seen in both bitches never bred from and those bred from early in life. The cause is an imbalance of the hormones that prepare the lining of the uterus for puppies so that fluid and mucus accumulates, leading to an acute illness if bacteria invade the organ.

It is known as 'open pyometra' when a blood-stained mucoid discharge comes out, often sticking to the hairs around the vulva; it has been confused with a bitch coming on heat unexpectedly. It can be more difficult to diagnose the cause of illness when there is no discharge present, known as a 'closed pyometra'. Other ways of testing the patient for the uterus disorder may be employed by the vet. Although medical treatments are available, it is more usual to perform a hysterectomy, especially if the bitch has come to the end of her breeding career.

RABIES

The fatal virus infection is almost unknown in the UK, but it remains as a cause of death of animals and humans in parts of the world where the preventive vaccine is not in regular use. The disease attacks a dog's central nervous system; it is spread by infective saliva and usually follows after the bite of an animal developing the disease. Annual rabies vaccination is an important way of controlling the disease.

We are fortunate that the West Highland White Terrier is a hardy breed and suffers from few inherited disorders.

RINGWORM

Ringworm is a fungus disease of the skin that has nothing to do with worms, but it acquired the name from the circular red marks on the skin following infection. It may appear as bald, scaly patches and will spread to children or adults handling the dog unless precautions are taken. Treatments will vary depending on the extent of the problem; painting a small area with povidone-iodine repeatedly can be effective, as can an all-over wash with a fungicide applied every three days. Another method is to dose the dog with Griseofulvin tablets for three to four weeks; it should not be used if either the bitch or handler are pregnant.

VESTIBULAR DISEASE

The older Westie may be subject to a head tilt, often with the eye-flicking movements known as nystagmus. At one time it was commonly diagnosed as a 'stroke', because of its suddenness; the dog may circle or fall on one side, rolling as he cannot balance. Vestibular disease develops suddenly, but unlike the equivalent human stroke, there is no sign of bleeding or of a vascular accident in the brain. Recovery is slow, as the balance centre of the brain regains its use after one to three weeks. Treatment by the vet will assist a return to normal, although some dogs always carry their head with a tilt. Where the head tilt persists or signs get worse, a specialist investigation may be needed to detect an inner ear disease infection or a brain tumour.

INHERITED DISORDERS

Genetic defects and disorders have been a problem for a long time, but improved veterinary diagnostic methods and the fact that dogs live longer make it more likely that degenerative diseases are able to show themselves. Healthy parents should always be selected when breeding.

CLEFT PALATE

Cleft palate among Westies is not a major breed problem, but the abnormality is seen from time to time in newborn puppies who have obvious difficulty in feeding when sucking the mother's milk. The condition allows food or fluid to enter the nasal respiratory passage and is often associated with the more obvious 'hare lip' where the two sides of the upper lips have failed to join while the embryo was developing in the uterus.

Increasingly, owners are becoming aware of the benefit of complementary therapies.

EYE CONDITIONS

Cataracts may occur in some puppies; after they open their eyelids they seem blind, having white opaque lenses. In older dogs the lens may become loose, causing loss of sight, this is known as 'lens luxation', but is more common in terrier breeds. Entropion as an abnormality of the eyelids is seen in the younger dog as an inward turning of the lid, the lashes rub on the eyeball surface (the cornea), causing irritation and eye watering. Conditions that affect the inside of the eye are more serious and can lead to blindness, as the retina is the most important site of disease in the eye. Although uncommon, there is a group of inherited diseases known as progressive retinal atrophy (PRA), which are known to occur in certain families. Retinal dysplasia (RD) is another abnormality found only rarely, and the condition known as lens luxation, leading to loss of sight in one eye, is now very uncommon.

PATELLAR LUXATION

The slipping out of place of the kneecap is often an inherited disease in smaller breeds, but it may also be the result of a torn ligament after jumping. Westies may be affected when they seem to move normally, then start limping on a back leg – sometimes so much that the affected leg is held up; the hock is rotated outwards, as the patellar is out of its normal groove, slipping inwardly (medial). The condition is not painful and gently bending up the leg may unlock the patellar so it slips back into the correct place. Surgical operations are quite successful in curing the condition.

PYRUVATE KINASE DEFICIENCY

This disease affects West Highland White Terriers, causing anaemia and disorders of the bone marrow and liver. It is extremely rare and is due to a deficiency of an enzyme in the red blood cells and can be diagnosed only after blood tests are performed. Tests can now be carried out on the DNA from blood samples and the defective gene identified – another example of modern technology being used to identify inherited disorders.

SKIN DISORDERS

The study of the possible inherited basis of skin problems is of increasing importance, of which the West Highland White Terrier has received some attention. Chronic disorders such as atopic dermatitis, primary seborrhoea and contact dermatitis may be linked to an abnormality in the immune system of the dog. Treatment of individual Westies is often effective, but prolonged medication may be required.

UMBILICAL HERNIA

Operations on young puppies to correct a bulge in the 'belly button' are sometimes required. It is a fairly minor procedure, but the condition should be watched for when purchasing a puppy.

COMPLEMENTARY THERAPIES

There is a wide choice of

treatments that can be given to dogs over and above the type of medical or surgical treatment that you might expect when attending a veterinary surgery. Some of these alternative treatments have proved to benefit dogs while others are better known for their effect on humans, where the placebo effect of an additional therapy has a strong influence on the benefit received.

Physiotherapy: This is one of the longest tested treatments used in injuries and after surgery on the limbs. Chartered physiotherapists and veterinary nurses who have studied the subject work under the direction of the vet and advise or apply procedures that will help mobility and recovery. Massage, heat, exercise or electrical stimulation are used to relieve pain, regain movement and restore muscle strength.

Hydrotherapy: This is very popular, as many dogs enjoy swimming, and the use of water for the treatment of joint disease, injuries or for the maintenance of fitness and health is very effective.

Acupuncture: Derived from Chinese medicine, with a long history of healing, acupuncture involves the insertion of fine needles into specific locations in the body, known as 'acupuncture points'. The placing of the needles to stimulate nervous tissue is based on human charts and very good results have been reported when veterinary acupuncturists have selected suitable cases to treat.

Reiki: The laying on of a skilled

With good care and management, your Westie should live a long, happy and healthy life.

operator's hands can have beneficial results; it is as equally convincing as acupuncture, and does not involve the dog tolerating needles in its body, but there are few qualified veterinary operators.

Magnetic therapy: Perhaps more questionable in observed results, magnetic therapy involves applying magnetic products to the dog, to relieve pain and increase mobility.

Aromatherapy: Also having a following, aromatherapy involves the treatment of dogs with natural remedies, essential oils and plant extracts, traditionally found in the wild.

Phytotherapy: Herbal medicine has proven benefits and there are an ever increasing number of veterinary surgeons skilled in selecting appropriate plant products. Natural remedies are attractive to many users and provide a good alternative to a

number of conventional veterinary treatments. Herbal drugs have become increasingly popular and their use is widespread, but licensing regulations and studies on interactions between herbal products and other veterinary medicines are still incomplete. One treatment for kennel cough with liquorice, thyme and echinacea, helped to cure a dog in 24 hours without antibiotics.

As with all alternative therapies, it is necessary to consult a person who has the experience and specialised knowledge of applying the treatments. The Westie's own vet should be informed, since there are contradictions between some veterinary medicines and other remedies. Acute and/or chronic liver damage occurred after ingestion of some Chinese herbs and care in the application of 'natural products' is advised.

THE CONTRIBUTORS

THE EDITOR
GEOFF CORISH

Geoff Corish is a well-known figure in the dog world. He began in Westies when he was 16 years old and in his first ever litter he bred his first Champion, Sealaw Selena. From then on he went on to to handle over 30 Westie Champions alone and of those Ch Dianthus Button went on to Best in Show at Crufts in 1976. He branched out into other breeds and has handled literally hundreds of Champions of different breeds. In 1984 he handled his second Crufts Best in Show winner, which was the Lhasa Apso Ch. Saxonsprings Hackensack. Then came the most famous show dog of all time, Ch Saxonsprings Fresno, another Lhasa Apso. She was voted, by a panel of top judges, the dog of the 80s. She then came into the ownership of Geoff and from there he has bred five generations of Sealaw Champions. Geoff has judged at Crufts several times and in 2000 judged the terrier group. He has also judged Westies there and has judged in all parts of the world.
See Chapter Seven: The Perfect West Highland White Terrier.

JANE (HANNEKE) KABEL(Llovall)

Jane's first connection with West Highland White Terriers was in 1969 when she was still living in Holland – and she has never been without a Westie since. In 1973 she went to work in the Lasara kennel in the UK to learn how to trim Westies. She loved what she saw and bought a puppy from Mrs Graham, named Fun. In 1976 Jane took Dutch, Int. Ch. Lasara Lots of Fun and went to live with the Graham family, where she became a partner in the Lasara kennel. They bred several Champions before Jane returned to Holland. There, she showed Ch. Lasara Love All with great success, as well as breeding and showing two Dutch Champions. In 1999 Jane returned to the UK, and is very much enjoying being part of the dog scene here. Today, Jane is breeding under the Llovall prefix and continues to exhibit

and judge West Highland White Terriers.
See Chapter One: Getting to Know the West Highland White Terrier and Chapter Four: The New Arrival

ROBERT HILL (Olton)

Robert has been breeding and showing West Highland White Terriers for more than 30 years under the Olton affix. There are Olton Champions in the UK, Scandinavia and Canada. He is the archivist of The West Highland White Terrier Club of England and was made an honorary life member of the club in 2007.

He is the co-author of *An Illustrated History of One Hundred Years of the WHWT* published to commemorate the centenary of the breed in 2006. Robert is a Championship show judge of the breed and has officiated in many countries.
See Chapter Two: The First West Highland White Terriers.

DOT BRITTEN (Krisma)

Dot's first West Highland White Terrier was a bitch bought in 1980 as a family pet, which was greatly loved. When Dot's family decided to add another Westie to the family, they wanted a dog they could show in a small way. Dot spent a lot of time going to shows, watching and trying to learn more about the breed.

Eventually, Dot was lucky enough to buy an eight-week-old bitch puppy from the Lasara Kennel that became her first Champion. She was a lovely example of the breed and is behind every pedigree of Dot's Krisma westies today. Since then, Dot has gone on to breed many more Champions. Her favourite homebred Champion is Ch. Krisma Streetwise, who has sired a number of Champions in the breed and was Westie Dog of the Year at the age of nine. Dot judges at Championship level in the UK and overseas.
See Chapter Three: A Westie for your Lifestyle.

DOREEN LANCASTER (Clanestar)

Doreen started in West Highland White Terriers in 1971. Like most

people, she bought a puppy as a pet for the family and then got 'hooked', showing the dog at local shows. Doreen then bought a bitch puppy from the Birkfell kennel, which she made into a Champion. This bitch won six Challenge Certificates and the Terrier Group at the Welsh Kennel Club show the day she became a Champion. Doreen has now made up a total of six Champions, and several Westies of her breeding have attained their titles abroad. Virtually every Westie Doreen has shown has gained a Stud Book number and/or Junior Warrant. She now runs a small kennel, specialising in breeding for temperament and good health.

Doreen did not start judging until she had been in the breed for 15 years or more, as she much preferred exhibiting. However, she has judged at Championship level for a few years, both home and abroad, including Sweden, France, Italy and Australia.
See Chapter Five: The Best of Care.

JULIA BARNES

Julia has owned and trained a number of different dog breeds, and is a puppy socialiser for Dogs for the Disabled. A former journalist, she has written many books, including several on dog training and behaviour. Julia is indebted to TINA SQUIRES (Bellevue) for her specialist knowledge of West highland White Terriers.
See Chapter Six: Training and Socialisation

DICK LANE BScFRAgSFRCVS

Dick qualified from the Royal Veterinary College in 1953 and then spent most of his time in veterinary practice in Warwickshire. He had a particular interest in assistance dogs: working for the Guide Dogs for the Blind Association and more recently for Dogs for the Disabled as a founder Trustee. Dick has been awarded a Fellowship of the Royal College of Veterinary Surgeons and a Fellowship of the Royal Agricultural Societies. He has recently completed an Honours BSc in Applied Animal Behaviour and Training, awarded by the University of Hull.
See Chapter Eight: Happy and Healthy.

USEFUL ADDRESSES

KENNEL & BREED CLUBS

UK
The Kennel Club
1 Clarges Street, London, W1J 8AB
Tel: 0870 606 6750
Fax: 0207 518 1058
Web: www.the-kennel-club.org.uk

To obtain up-to-date contact information for the following breed clubs, contact the Kennel Club:
• North of Ireland West Highland White Terrier Club
• Southern West Highland White Terrier Club
• West Highland White Terrier Club
• West Highland White Terrier Club of England
• West Highland White Terrier Club of Wales

USA
American Kennel Club (AKC)
5580 Centerview Drive,
Raleigh, NC 27606, USA.
Tel: 919 233 9767
Fax: 919 233 3627
Email: info@akc.org
Web: www.akc.org

United Kennel Club (UKC)
100 E Kilgore Rd, Kalamazoo,
MI 49002-5584, USA.
Tel: 269 343 9020
Fax: 269 343 7037
Web:www.ukcdogs.com/

West Highland White Terrier Club of America, Inc.
Web: http://www.westieclubamerica.com/

For contact details of regional clubs, please contact The West Highland White Terrier Club of America.

AUSTRALIA
Australian National Kennel Council (ANKC)
The Australian National Kennel Council is the administrative body for pure breed canine affairs in Australia. It does not, however, deal directly with dog exhibitors, breeders or judges. For information pertaining to breeders, clubs or shows, please contact the relevant State or Territory Controlling Body.

Dogs Australian Capital Teritory
PO Box 815, Dickson ACT 2602
Tel: (02) 6241 4404
Fax: (02) 6241 1129
Email: administrator@dogsact.org.au
Web: www.dogsact.org.au

Dogs New South Wales
PO Box 632, St Marys, NSW 1790
Tel: (02) 9834 3022 or 1300 728 022 (NSW Only)
Fax: (02) 9834 3872
Email: info@dogsnsw.org.au
Web: www.dogsnsw.org.au

Dogs Northern Territory
PO Box 37521, Winnellie NT 0821
Tel: (08) 8984 3570
Fax: (08) 8984 3409
Email: admin@dogsnt.com.au
Web: www.dogsnt.com.au

Dogs Queensland
PO Box 495, Fortitude Valley Qld 4006
Tel: (07) 3252 2661
Fax: (07) 3252 3864
Email: info@dogsqueensland.org.au
Web: www.dogsqueensland.org.au

Dogs South Australia
PO Box 844
Prospect East SA 5082
Tel: (08) 8349 4797
Fax: (08) 8262 5751
Email: info@dogssa.com.au
Web: www.dogssa.com.au

Tasmanian Canine Association Inc
The Rothman Building
PO Box 116
Glenorchy Tas 7010
Tel: (03) 6272 9443
Fax: (03) 6273 0844
Email: tca@iprimus.com.au
Web: www.tasdogs.com

Dogs Victoria
Locked Bag K9
Cranbourne VIC 3977
Tel: (03)9788 2500
Fax: (03) 9788 2599
Email: office@dogsvictoria.org.au
Web: www.dogsvictoria.org.au

Dogs Western Australia
PO Box 1404
Canning Vale WA 6970
Tel: (08) 9455 1188
Fax: (08) 9455 1190
Email: k9@dogswest.com
Web: www.dogswest.com

INTERNATIONAL
Fédération Cynologique Internationalé (FCI)/World Canine Organisation
Place Albert 1er, 13, B-6530 Thuin, Belgium.
Tel: +32 71 59.12.38
Fax: +32 71 59.22.29
Web: www.fci.be/

TRAINING AND BEHAVIOUR

UK
Association of Pet Dog Trainers
PO Box 17, Kempsford, GL7 4WZ
Telephone: 01285 810811
Email: APDToffice@aol.com
Web: http://www.apdt.co.uk

Association of Pet Behaviour Counsellors
PO BOX 46, Worcester, WR8 9YS
Telephone: 01386 751151
Fax: 01386 750743
Email: info@apbc.org.uk
Web: http://www.apbc.org.uk/

USA
Association of Pet Dog Trainers
101 North Main Street, Suite 610
Greenville, SC 29601, USA.
Tel: 1 800 738 3647
Email: information@apdt.com
Web: www.apdt.com/

American College of Veterinary Behaviorists
College of Veterinary Medicine, 4474 Tamu, Texas A&M University
College Station, Texas 77843-4474
Web: http://dacvb.org/

American Veterinary Society of Animal Behavior
Web: www.avsabonline.org/

AUSTRALIA
APDT Australia Inc
PO Box 3122, Bankstown Square, NSW 2200,
Email: secretary@apdt.com.au
Web: www.apdt.com.au

Canine Behaviour
For details of regional behvaiourists, contact the relevant State or Territory Controlling Body.

ACTIVITIES

UK
Agility Club
http://www.agilityclub.co.uk/

British Flyball Association
PO Box 990, Doncaster, DN1 9FY
Telephone: 01628 829623
Email: secretary@flyball.org.uk
Web: http://www.flyball.org.uk/

USA
North American Dog Agility Council
P.O. Box 1206, Colbert,
OK 74733, USA.
Web: www.nadac.com/

North American Flyball Association, Inc.
1333 West Devon Avenue, #512
Chicago, IL 60660
Tel/Fax: 800 318 6312
Email: flyball@flyball.org
Web: www.flyball.org/

AUSTRALIA
Agility Dog Association of Australia
ADAA Secretary, PO Box 2212,
Gailes, QLD 4300, Australia.
Tel: 0423 138 914

Email: admin@adaa.com.au
Web: www.adaa.com.au/

NADAC Australia (North American Dog Agility Council - Australian Division)
12 Wellman Street, Box Hill South, Victoria 3128, Australia.
Email: shirlene@nadacaustralia.com
Web: www.nadacaustralia.com/

Australian Flyball Association
PO Box 4179, Pitt Town, NSW 2756
Tel: 0407 337 939
Email: info@flyball.org.au
Web: www.flyball.org.au/

INTERNATIONAL

World Canine Freestyle Organisation
P.O. Box 350122, Brooklyn, NY 11235-2525, USA
Tel: (718) 332-8336
Fax: (718) 646-2686
Email: wcfodogs@aol.com
Web: www.worldcaninefreestyle.org

HEALTH

UK

Alternative Veterinary Medicine Centre
Chinham House, Stanford in the Vale, Oxfordshire, SN7 8NQ
Tel: 01367 710324
Fax: 01367 718243
Web: www.alternativevet.org/

British Small Animal Veterinary Association
Woodrow House, 1 Telford Way, Waterwells Business Park, Quedgeley, Gloucestershire, GL2 2AB
Tel: 01452 726700
Fax: 01452 726701
Email: customerservices@bsava.com
Web: http://www.bsava.com/

Royal College of Veterinary Surgeons
Belgravia House, 62-64 Horseferry Road, London, SW1P 2AF
Tel: 0207 222 2001
Fax: 0207 222 2004
Email: admin@rcvs.org.uk
Web: www.rcvs.org.uk

USA

American Holistic Veterinary Medical Association
2218 Old Emmorton Road, Bel Air, MD 21015
Tel: 410 569 0795
Fax 410 569 2346
Email: office@ahvma.org
Web: www.ahvma.org/

American Veterinary Medical Association
1931 North Meacham Road, Suite 100, Schaumburg, IL 60173-4360, USA.
Tel: 800 248 2862
Fax: 847 925 1329
Web: www.avma.org

American College of Veterinary Surgeons
19785 Crystal Rock Dr, Suite 305
Germantown, MD 20874, USA.
Tel: 301 916 0200
Toll Free: 877 217 2287
Fax: 301 916 2287
Email: acvs@acvs.org
Web: www.acvs.org/

AUSTRALIA
Australian Holistic Vets
Web: www.ahv.com.au/

Australian Small Animal Veterinary Association
40/6 Herbert Street, St Leonards, NSW 2065, Australia.
Tel: 02 9431 5090
Fax: 02 9437 9068
Email: asava@ava.com.au
Web: www.asava.com.au

Australian Veterinary Association
Unit 40, 6 Herbert Street, St Leonards, NSW 2065, Australia.
Tel: 02 9431 5000
Fax: 02 9437 9068
Web: www.ava.com.au

Australian College Veterinary Scientists
Building 3, Garden City Office Park, 2404 Logan Road, Eight Mile Plains, Queensland 4113, Australia.
Tel: 07 3423 2016
Fax: 07 3423 2977
Email: admin@acvs.org.au
Web: http://acvsc.org.au

ASSISTANCE DOGS

UK
Canine Partners
Mill Lane, Heyshott, Midhurst, GU29 0ED
Tel: 08456 580480
Fax: 08456 580481
Web: www.caninepartners.co.uk

Dogs for the Disabled
The Frances Hay Centre, Blacklocks Hill, Banbury, Oxon, OX17 2BS
Tel: 01295 252600
Web: www.dogsforthedisabled.org

Guide Dogs for the Blind Association
Burghfield Common, Reading, RG7 3YG
Tel: 01189 835555
Fax: 01189 835433
Web: www.guidedogs.org.uk/

Hearing Dogs for Deaf People
The Grange, Wycombe Road, Saunderton, Princes Risborough, Bucks, HP27 9NS
Tel: 01844 348100
Fax: 01844 348101
Web: www.hearingdogs.org.uk

Pets as Therapy
14a High Street, Wendover, Aylesbury, Bucks. HP22 6EA.
Tel: 01845 345445
Fax: 01845 550236
Web: http://www.petsastherapy.org/

Support Dogs
21 Jessops Riverside, Brightside Lane, Sheffield, S9 2RX
Tel: 01142 617800
Fax: 01142 617555
Email: supportdogs@btconnect.com
Web: www.support-dogs.org.uk

USA
Therapy Dogs International
88 Bartley Road, Flanders, NJ 07836,.
Tel: 973 252 9800
Fax: 973 252 7171
Web: www.tdi-dog.o

Therapy Dogs Inc.
P.O. Box 20227, Cheyenne, WY 82003.
Tel: 307 432 0272.
Fax: 307-638-2079
Web: www.therapydogs.com

Delta Society - Pet Partners
875 124th Ave NE, Suite 101, Bellevue, WA 98005 USA.
Email: info@DeltaSociety.org
Web: www.deltasociety.org

Comfort Caring Canines
8135 Lare Street, Philadelphia, PA 19128.
Email: ccc@comfortcaringcanines.org
Web: www.comfortcaringcanines.org/

AUSTRALIA
AWARE Dogs Australia, Inc
PO Box 883, Kuranda, Queensland, 488..
Tel: 07 4093 8152
Web: www.awaredogs.org.au/

Delta Society — Therapy Dogs
Web: www.deltasociety.com.au